PRAISE FOR DON'T FEAR THE SHARKS

"I was blessed to have gone onto Shark Tank and receive an investment from Mr. Wonderful (Kevin O'Leary). However, reading, learning, and implementing the best practices & pitfalls to avoid from *Don't Fear The Sharks* would have saved countless hours, time, and energy in my preparation to secure funding."
  – Brian Brasch, CEO, PRX Performance

"It has been a joy to watch Kelvin courageously lead his company from inception to now. Both Kelvin and Brevity are light years ahead from where they started. It's clear that those learnings and insights can help entrepreneurs shorten the time it takes for them to raise capital they need and at more favorable terms. I encourage entrepreneurs to read this book before raising capital."
  – Mary MacCarthy, Senior Program Manager/
    Discovery Capital Manager, Venture Center,
    University of Minnesota

"For any first-time founder in the initial stages of launching a company, *Don't Fear The Sharks* is must read. Reading this book along with leveraging Brevity's software will give you mindset, belief system, and guidance to persuade and influence investors and customers."
  – Katherine Johnson, Chief People & Legal Officer, Storj

"I've seen Kelvin develop as a leader, entrepreneur, and sales professional over the past seven years. I'm amazed by his development but more impressed with the actionable insights he poured into *Don't Fear the Sharks*. When I started my first two companies, this book would have saved me time, heartache, and provided the inspiration needed when faced with rejection from prospective investors and clients."

– Wade Rosen, CEO, Atari

Don't Fear the Sharks

Don't Fear the Sharks: Six Principles to Pitch Investors

Copyright © 2023 by Kelvin Johnson
All rights reserved. No part of this book may be reproduced or used in any manner without the prior written permission of the copyright holder, except for the use of brief quotations in a book review.

ISBN 978-1-948529-18-1 (paperback)
ISBN 978-1-948529-21-1 (ePub)
Library of Congress Control Number: 2023905783

Edited by LaToya Taris-James
Book and Cover Design by Paul Nylander | Illustrada

Strive Publishing
Robbinsdale, Minnesota

Contents

Inspiration 1
Introduction: Learning from Failure 9

Principle 1: Validate your key assumptions 13
   Beth Fynbo, CEO & Founder of Busy Baby 15
   Katy Mallory, CEO & Co-Founder of Slumberpod 18
   Becca Davison, CEO & Co-Founder of Unbuckleme 21

Principle 2: Anticipate the Post Pitch 25
   Katy Mallory, CEO & Co-Founder, Slumberpod 27
   Brian Brasch, CEO & Co-Founder of PrX Performance .. 28
      TABLE 1: BRIAN BRASCH (BB) AND ERIK HOPPERSTAD (EH)
      POST-PITCH QUESTIONS 31
   Robbie Cordo, Entrepreneur Coach 33
      TABLE 2: ROBBIE CORDO INSPIRED POST-PITCH TOOL 34
   Brevity's Anticipation Questions & Process 38

Principle 3: Know Your Audience 43
   Our Approach to the Friends & Family Round 47
   Best Practices & Lessons Learned from Friends & Family Round 49
   Targeting for our $1M Round & Process 51

Principle 4: Incorporate Your Motivation 61
   Cultivate relationships with people who believe in you . . . 69
   Cultivate a healthy relationship with your body & mind . . 70

Principle 5: Pitching is a numbers game 81
   Brian Brasch, CEO & Co-Founder at PrX Performance . . . 86
   Beth Fynbo, CEO & Founder of Busy Baby 86
   Tripp Phillips: Co-Founder of Le-Glue 87
   Katy Mallory, CEO & Co-Founder at Slumberpod 87
   Becca Davison, CEO & Co-Founder at UnbuckleMe 88

Principle 6: Make sure your pitch has SOUL™ 91
   S: STATE TARGET AUDIENCE & PROBLEM 94
   Kyndo, Kelly McDonald, 500 Startups Demo Day 94
   Laura Musall, CEO, Cool Revolution, 2-Minute Drill Pitch 95
   Ryan Sydnor, CEO, Get Grow, 500 Startups Demo Day . . 96
   Devon Copley, CEO, Avatour, 500 Startups Demo Day . . . 98
   Anton Brevde, CEO, Asseta, Y-Combinator Demo Day . . 99
   Kelvin Johnson Jr., CEO & Co-Founder Brevity 100

CONTENTS

O: OUTLINE HOW & WHY YOUR SOLUTION WORKS 102
- Kyndo, Kelly McDonald, 500 Startups Demo Day 103
- Laura Musall, CEO, Cool Revolution, 2-Minute Drill Pitch 104
- Ryan Sydnor, CEO, Get Grow, 500 Startups Demo Day . 105
- Devon Copley, CEO, Avatour, 500 Startups Demo Day.. 106
- Anton Brevde, CEO, Asseta, Y-Combinator Demo Day . 107
- Kelvin Johnson, CEO & Co-Founder of Brevity 109

U: UNCOVER PROOF & POTENTIAL 110
- Kyndo, Kelly McDonald, 500 Startups Demo Day 111
- Laura Musall, CEO, Cool Revolution, 2-Minute Drill Pitch 113
- Ryan Sydnor, CEO, Get Grow, 500 Startups Demo Day . 114
- Devon Copley, CEO, Avatour, 500 Startups Demo Day.. 116
- Anton Brevde, CEO, Asseta, Y-Combinator Demo Day . 117
- Kelvin Johnson, CEO & Co-Founder of Brevity 118

L: LIST CAPABILITIES & NEEDS 120
- Kyndo, Kelly McDonald, 500 Startups Demo Day 121
- Laura Musall, CEO, Cool Revolution, 2-Minute Drill Pitch 124
- Ryan Sydnor, CEO, Get Grow, 500 Startups Demo Day . 124
- Devon Copley, CEO, Avatour, 500 Startups Demo Day.. 125
- Kelvin Johnson, CEO & Co-Founder of Brevity 127

NOW WHAT? 128

Outro & Additional Resources 129

References 131

Inspiration

I grew up in West Philadelphia, a talkative child of two sales professionals. My dad had been selling technology for the last forty years of his career, and my mom was a pharmaceutical Rep for Johnson & Johnson. You could definitely say my parents' business acumen rubbed off on me. I've always kept journals of business ideas and inventions, even as a child. One of my favorites was called the "Ultimate Channel Surfing Device," a device that reminded you when your favorite show returned from a commercial break. It allowed one to channel surf during commercials with peace of mind. When I decided to pursue accounting and become a Certified Public Accountant (CPA) as my first job, they were perplexed. I'm sure their thoughts were, "How the hell are you gonna be a CPA if you can't stop running your mouth?" They were right. That career was short-lived. I couldn't see myself working in Microsoft Excel for twelve hours a day, and above all, I just didn't feel fulfilled.

After being a CPA at Ernst and Young for a year, I was at a crossroads in my career, so I decided to put my gift of gab to good use and pursue a career in management consulting. I guess I really do have a gift because I landed at a Top 20 management consulting firm in New York City. I thought this was a better mix of salesmanship and analytics. I loved that career and got a strong foundation there. I learned how to be hypothesis-driven, synthesize data, and provide recommendations to clients to make their operations and strategies more effective and efficient.

These are all essential skills when analyzing complex problems, which helped me in my later business ventures. A quote I've always loved, and is often attributed to Charles Kettering of General Motors, is "A problem well defined is half solved." This quote is especially true in consulting, but also explains the larger theme of my journey. One of seeking and defining and finding. I knew in consulting that I had only half solved my puzzle.

When I look back on my life experiences, I'm proud that I proved to myself that I had the discipline to stick with things which may not be my end goal but surely would help me get where I wanted to go—obtaining a CPA license and finding success in management consulting. But I still felt a draw toward something else. I was at another crossroads in my career and thought I should be making more money by now. At this point, I thought I could do one of two things, go to the dark side (sales), which my parents have done for most of their careers, or take a position where I can see more of my ideas come to fruition and see myself grow even more. I chose the latter and became the fifth employee of the tech company in Denver, CO, called ThrivePass.

ThrivePass is a corporate wellness software corporation and (knock on wood) the second-best decision I made in my career. I was Director of Operations, managing the operations team in Denver and a team of ten .NET Developers in New Delhi, India. I was responsible for account management and customer success. I also built financial models and a new business unit from the ground up. That was my very first project.

The best thing about that opportunity versus my other corporate experiences was that I was encouraged to be myself. In a corporate setting there are a lot of obstacles and distractions that Black people especially face. We adapt by code-switching and playing into respectability politics, fitting into the mold of how these spaces define professionalism. I appreciated that this was one place where I didn't have to wear a three-piece suit or talk a certain way to be taken seriously. I recognized that this was the culture and environment in which I worked best—rapid, fast-paced, and able to quickly implement ideas, whereas in consulting, I felt like I had to work for approvals just to go to the restroom. This was where I learned the importance of truly bringing my whole self to work, and I thrived.

I knew that at that point, I wanted to not only stay in this type of environment but eventually run a company that embodies this type of culture of my own. The CEO and Founder of that company, Wade Rosen told me early in my career that I had the makings of a CEO and if I had a legitimate business idea down the line that he would invest in me, he ended up keeping that promise.

As a first-time Co-Founder who raised a "friends and family" round of $232,150 in 2021, I never went through anything more grueling and rewarding in my career. Even as I wrote this book, my company, Brevity (brevitypitch.com), was in the middle of a $1M capital raise which has shown not to be any easier. We get to why raising capital is challenging later in the book and provide pivotal lessons learned in hindsight. It has always been on my bucket list to write a book, but when I did, I wanted it to be meaningful, to chronicle my journey and what I learned, and to be written with brevity (no pun intended).

I was always told that you needed to enjoy the arduous process on your path to greatness. One of my former bosses in my consulting career, Christopher Sicuranza, told me you need to *embrace the suck*. Before starting a company of my own, it was easy to criticize what previous CEOs could be doing better and differently. My perspective changed once I actually got into the CEO & Co-Founder seat. Getting firsthand experience on how taxing it is to run your own business took me by surprise. One of the biggest challenges in the early stages was the amount of context switching from activities you enjoy to ones you dread. This ranged from handling compliance issues, conversations with various attorneys, partnership challenges, sales opportunities, and the biggest beast of them all—raising capital from investors. In 2021 alone, we pitched over 130 investors and landed 16 investors for our cap table.

In writing this book, I wanted to provide inspiration and insight to others facing similar challenges and opportunities as startup founders and anyone out there pitching. One day I was listening to a playlist. The song, "Don't Fear the Reaper" by Blue Oyster Cult came on, and the idea for this book, *Don't Fear the Sharks: Six Principles to Pitch Investors*—came to life. During my journey of pitching, I recognize how significant clarity, connection, confidence, and conviction are essential ingredients to accomplishing your fundraising goals. Fear can either be fuel or, if not properly processed, interference. Part of the goal of this book is to provide you with actionable steps to overcome fears when pitching and performing as your best self.

I'd like to give you some background on my company, Brevity. Brevity is an AI-powered software helping professionals craft and deliver persuasive pitches and presentations that sell. Our software is ideal for a wide variety of high-stakes professional communication scenarios, including but not limited to raising capital, growing sales, internal corporate presentations, interview preparation, and much more. When pitching a business, some external factors are outside one's control. You're in competition against shrinking attention spans, low comprehension rates, and Zoom fatigue. As a result, people have less time and patience to clarify what you presented. In the world of pitching, when you confuse your audience, you lose. The goal of Brevity is to help your pitch be easy to understand and compelling, driving your target audience to want to learn more. The six principles in this book give you conceptual knowledge. If you wish to take your pitch further, Brevity the software can help you craft and deliver a clear, concise, and compelling pitch and presentation to drive your amazing ideas to success.

There are details and nuances this book does not cover. One of our best analogies to explain how our software works is to think about how TurboTax makes filing taxes easier for the everyday person. Instead of paying for an expensive expert, TurboTax provides an affordable solution with an easily used interface with digestible steps and concrete examples throughout the process. Brevity mirrors a similar concept in terms of being quick, easy, and powerful. So, when you have that groundbreaking idea, Brevity walks you down the yellow brick road reducing the cognitive load to craft and deliver a compelling pitch and presentation. Review our video *How Brevity Works* at www.youtube.com/watch?v=WEeJPI0f4Nk.

In this book I'm explaining Brevity's critical concepts and foundational principles and what made us successful in raising capital. I will provide inspirational stories and examples from exceptional founders we know intimately. I hope you enjoy this material. By the end of it, you should walk away with insights and inspiration, knowing you can successfully pitch investors. Most importantly, you will build a belief system and you won't fear the sharks!

Introduction: Learning from Failure

It was a cold Minneapolis winter night, and I was on the way to meet Wade Rosen, CEO of Atari & previous boss at a startup ThrivePass where I was an executive leadership team member. Wade always thought that I had the makings of CEO, and during my time at ThrivePass, he said he would proudly fund my first startup venture should I decide to take that leap. His biggest prerequisite was that it had to be an idea he believed in and that I was mature enough to steer that ship. At the time, he was already aware and excited about my idea, which was the basis for Brevity, my current company.

When I was ready to pitch him formally, I met him for dinner and drinks at a spot we usually hit called George and the Dragon in East Harriet, Minneapolis. My former boss has what everyone calls the gift of gab. He is very charismatic and makes everyone feel comfortable (unless he's pissed at you). We began the conversation by landing on a random topic and concept like, "Why is the public education system in the Twin Cities better than other cities?" As I was trying to land my first big investment for my new venture, I was okay with the way the conversation flowed, as long as I was confident and ready to make the *BIG ASK* of $250K to build Brevity.

After we ordered a few drinks and finished some appetizers, I felt like I was ready to ask for $250K for investment into Brevity. However, Wade Rosen beat me to the punch and said, "How are things going with Brevity?" At the time, we'd hired a new team member and were still finalizing the first version of our product. I became a little nervous when he asked this.

To prep for this dinner with Wade, I worked with a mentor who suggested I go into it believing that *I* was the one who was doing *him* a favor. That's the confidence you need to demonstrate in these situations. Conviction in the early stages of startup investing is one of the key ingredients to securing funding. I believe this principle in concept, but of course it can be difficult to implement in real life without much experience.

So, I attempted to communicate our progress but quickly jumped to "we need an investment of $250K from you," followed by telling him that another prospective investor said if he invested $250K, he would match that investment. I thought this was the hook and it would be a no-brainer for Wade to write the check instantly. I was sadly mistaken.

Suddenly he thanked me for considering him as an investor, and the topic turned from Brevity to a slew of unrelated topics. However, the fifth topic somehow tied to the overall sentiment of "What are the key assumptions of your model? Have you validated these assumptions?"

I was puzzled and shocked that he was going so hard on me. My mind was on fire ... *wtf dude?! Your word was that you would fund me once I found a great idea for a business, and I was mature enough. What went wrong here? Do you not have the money you said you did?*

Wade stopped and said, "When you validate these assumptions, then I will gladly write you a check."

I had concerns. I told Wade that my lead developer couldn't live without a paycheck for too long and asked what to say to the other investor who offered to match the investment? Wade looked me in my eyes saying, "That's your job to figure out."

The moral of the story, and one of the key principles of this book, is to validate key assumptions before ever diving into a pitch for investment. This book will spotlight a variety of entrepreneurs on their journeys to discovering, launching, and pitching a business that will get funded by shark tank-like investors, institutional funds, and angel investors. We hope you will find insight as you think about starting, funding, and growing your business.

The six core principles you will learn in each are:

1. Validate your key assumptions
2. Anticipate & prepare for the post-pitch
3. Know your audience
4. Incorporate your motivation
5. Pitching is a numbers game
6. Make sure your pitch has SOUL™

By the end of this book, we want you to walk away with inspiration, confidence, and pragmatic tips to pitch your business and win. We want to help you succeed!

Principle 1: Validate your key assumptions

Great ideas without substance, evidence, and proof will fall short. Your target audience needs qualitative and quantitative proof that what you're pitching will work, and that there are strong indicators that people will be willing to buy, and there are a lot of them. This step should be completed before you begin to think about pitching for money. Because you believe so strongly in the validity of your idea and your vision, this could be a tempting step to skip. It's time-consuming but will save you a ton of time, money, and heartache in the end.

> "What are your key assumptions? Have you validated them?"
>
> Wade Rosen, CEO of Atari

This principle can be the most challenging of them all. My Co-Founder and I conceptualized Brevity and thought artificial intelligence would help people craft a clear, concise, and compelling narrative. From this, we eventually ended up trademarking Brevity Pitch Intelligence.™ We thought, "This idea is a hit! What investor and customer wouldn't want to invest in or buy this product? We have something revolutionary that no one has ever done!"

But the assumption that was not validated was: does our product work, and would customers want to buy it? What type of customers would purchase it? Is Brevity just a one-time purchase or a recurring one? Is this a nice to have or a need to have? Is it a feature or a product? How big is the actual problem? Is the market big enough? Is there an actual demand? If you read the introduction, you know I learned a powerful lesson about validating assumptions. Honestly, it's a lesson I'm still learning and need constant reminders. Validating your assumptions is truly about your customer and not about you. This can be challenging for a person like me with a background in sales focused on trying to influence and persuade. It was always my job to identify pain and clearly demonstrate where our solution provides cost savings, return on investment (ROI), etc.

But startups are in a constant state of validation and recalibration. In this chapter, we will highlight concrete examples of where entrepreneurs we know did an exceptional job of validating the businesses, products, and customers. These validation methods not only made their pitch strong but, more importantly, demonstrated they have viable business models worth investment.

BETH FYNBO, CEO & FOUNDER OF BUSY BABY

Beth is a military veteran and entrepreneur from Minnesota who created a product many parents with babies could benefit from. Never imagining she'd become an entrepreneur, she always considered herself an effective problem solver. As a parent, she saw how her baby always threw things at the dinner table—toys, utensils, whatever was within reach—whether at home or in restaurants. Beth would become frustrated, embarrassed, and finally convinced that there had to be a better way. She was at her wits' end and began researching solutions to the problem. The operative word here is research!

Research Process

The last thing Beth had in mind was building a business. She was adamant about just fixing the problem at hand. So, how could she do this? She didn't want to reinvent the wheel, so she first needed to determine if there was already a solution to her problem. She searched extensively on Amazon with keywords, went to baby stores, and asked other mothers if they had experienced their babies throwing toys and utensils at the dinner table making a mess and how they handled it. Ultimately, she came up short and couldn't find anything to help her. Beth decided it was time to roll up her sleeves and reinvent the wheel.

Your functional prototype doesn't need to be pretty, but it should fix the pain. Once Beth realized there wasn't a functional product to help solve this problem, she set to building one herself. The solution she came up with was basically using string that connected to the mat so when the baby throws the toys and utensils they won't go beyond a certain distance. She went to various hardware stores and tried using silicon placemats (designed for cats & dogs), fishing tethers, and other material to build her first prototype. It wasn't pretty, but it got the job done. The toys and utensils were no longer being thrown off the table, and they could all finally enjoy family dinner.

> "When someone can't live without your product, you are on to something."
> Kelvin Johnson

Still not thinking about starting a business, Beth gave the prototype to one of her girlfriends with a baby. Her friend found it helpful. However, one day she brought her child to a bowling alley and forgot the prototype at home. Her child made a mess, and she told Beth she'd never again leave home without it. Here was the "aha!" moment that got Beth thinking there might be a real business opportunity here.

Your first investment testing the validity of your business may be smaller than you think. It took $1,000 for Beth to make her first real prototype and start taking it to trade shows. There she could see customer demand for her product up close and in person. Beth also joined Bunkerlabs (bunkerlabs.org), a program for military veterans to find resources and tools to help launch and grow their businesses.

Key Learnings
Beth validated her business in the following sequence: self, close friends, family, and eventually, trade shows. The sequence goes from lowest stakes (if it didn't work for Beth, she simply would have tried something else) to people who don't want to hurt your feelings (her friend) to others who can validate before you start pitching for customers and investors. It's tempting to believe you have an amazing idea, but you need to validate it by testing it in an environment that includes potential buyers in the market to see if your product is salable and might find success. Beth happened to receive an offer an offer on Shark Tank from Lori Greiner.

KATY MALLORY, CEO & CO-FOUNDER OF SLUMBERPOD

As Plato says, *necessity is the mother of invention*. Katy Mallory is an entrepreneur from Atlanta, Georgia who, like Beth Fynbo, proved that mothers are the mothers of invention too. Katy developed Slumberpod, a device that helps babies sleep well in new or different locations. She remembered how the idea was born. Katy took her family on vacation to visit her mom who had her other six kids and three stepchildren all together under one roof. (Her mother ultimately would become Co-Founder of Slumberpod, proving that two mothers of invention are better than one). While there, Katy and her husband shared a room with their 15-month-old daughter. Although Katy's daughter slept well at home, sleeping at Grandma's proved to be a challenge. The blinds let light in from the outside disrupting the baby's sleep. The energy of all those kids together in one house was not something Katy's baby was familiar with. When she finally did fall asleep, she woke up suddenly and saw her parents, then couldn't get back to sleep. She even hid under the covers, but that didn't help. The house was full, and there was nowhere else to go. She, her husband, and the baby were miserable, having come all this way for a happy getaway.

They woke up the next morning sleep-deprived, grumpy, and on edge. After two nights of this, they cut the trip short. They'd had such high hopes to create happy memories during their stay.

Their next thought was what this meant for future trips. How could they navigate this and find some relaxing family time to get away together? They knew there had to be a solution—some way for them all to get some sleep when staying away from home. Even without her mother's full house, Katy worried that her toddler's restless sleep would put the kibosh on anymore overnights. She also suspected they weren't the only parents facing this challenge. Like all new parents in the digital age, Katy ventured online to find out what others with the same problem had done.

Research Process
Katy researched all around for things like dark lighting and other possible solutions but kept coming up empty. Nothing seemed to be a solid fix for what they were facing. She tried making a tent using two cheap camera tripods with a sheet draped between them tethered to each with a ponytail holder and twist ties. That helped a bit at night but in the morning, sunlight would stream in through the curtains and sheets which meant an early wake-up for everyone. This was an improvement, but more work was needed.

Katy started talking to friends and family, asking if they also had this challenge. Katy knew that only talking to friends and family was only going to be a small sample size so they created a survey and asked their friends and family to forward to others who might have been having or have had the same problem.

Additionally, they joined mom groups on Facebook across the country and sent the other group members the survey. They had close to 700 responses and found out that 70% of respondents said their babies sleep incredibly well at home but struggle to sleep well away from home. They also held some focus groups to better understand if this was a true challenge. Furthermore, as a part of those focus groups, they talked about product features and pricing and what would be important to their target audience.

Katy also credits a lot of her early success to joining an accelerator program in Columbus, Georgia. Through the program, participants were required to hit milestones much faster than if they were doing it by themselves. For example, during the second class, the participants were asked to come up with a business canvas which consisted of their business plan and who their customer segments were. Other milestones included sales projections, descriptions of anticipated data research like focus groups, surveys, etc. These milestones were there to validate whether the entrepreneur has an idea that would stick. There were milestones which included listing out what might need intellectual property protection, like provisional patents, trademarks etc. The team at the accelerator that they joined helped them think through questions to ask in her surveys and focus groups. Additionally, they made it a goal to talk to two entrepreneurs a week. People were vulnerable and willing to help

Katy with best practices and pitfalls to avoid in many facets of starting and growing a company. They would send thank you notes with specific takeaways after each time they connected with other successful entrepreneurs.

BECCA DAVISON, CEO & CO-FOUNDER OF UNBUCKLEME

Becca Davison is an entrepreneur from Houston, Texas who started Unbuckleme with her mother, Barbara Heilman in 2016. Unbuckleme is a tool that makes it easier to unbuckle kids' car seats. Before becoming an entrepreneur, she worked in the corporate world as a management consultant. After having her first daughter, Becca wanted to make sure she spent a lot of time with grandma, but they quickly realized a major problem. Because of Becca's mother's arthritis, she couldn't unbuckle her car seat without a ton of pain. An occupational therapist by trade, Becca's mother quickly built a tool to solve her own problem.

Being in the industry for so long, it was natural for Becca's mother to think about solutions to maximize functionality within a patient's ability. She designed a little C-shaped tool that would reduce the force required to unbuckle a car seat (before it would take nine lbs.). Using a mix of materials that were in her garage, she built a tool within a week. To Becca's surprise and puzzlement, her mother casually mentioned that she solved the problem. When Becca saw the device, she realized her mother couldn't be the only one who had this problem and that it had the potential to become a company. Becca's mom originally offered to make a few more for Becca's friends. But Becca made it clear this was bigger than just a few friends—this was something they could actually manufacture and sell.

Validation & Research Approach

Becca and her mother decided to conduct market research to see if there was anything in the market for their problem. They went car seat shopping to see if they could find a buckle that was easier to open than the seat Becca had purchased for her daughter. They couldn't find one and with reason: you don't want kids unbuckling their car seats.

Part of Becca and her mother's research was asking questions like: "How many grandparents are taking care of kids?" They looked at census data, "How many people have arthritis?" They learned that it was the number one disability in America. They spoke with other parents, went to baby stores and car seat departments, and asked sales reps, "Do people complain about this issue?" Sales associates shared that people shop and complain about this problem constantly. Over time they realized there was an industry-specific trade show where they could validate if their product was an actual opportunity, learn how to bring a product like this to market, what customer segments would buy it, what does the supply chain look like. They hopped on a plane and went to Vegas. Media, buyers, and suppliers all loved the product from a business standpoint but, more importantly, had specific applications for their own aunts, uncles, and friends.

Additionally, they learned of new customer segments like people with long nails who also suffered from this problem.

One important note is that Becca and her mother filed patents before going to the trade show. For a product like this, it was important to file patents prior to protect their intellectual property. Another note is that they filed patents just with their prototypes. They eventually created fifty 3D-prototype prints and sent them out to strangers to get feedback. Becca highlights that it was nice to get friends' and family members' feedback but was another thing to receive feedback from people who didn't care about hurting your feelings. She asked them, "Tell me what you think. Would you buy this?" "What price would you be willing to pay? Is there anything you'd change about it?" The insights Becca received were incredibly valuable.

I wondered how she found those fifty people to send the prototypes and she said she had met someone at the trade show who works in media relations and had a large online following. That person posted a video of Becca's prototype which garnered about 16K views. In the comment sections, people went nuts with excitement, noting "I need this, I need this!!" When Becca returned home, she messaged each of those comments, and received fifty responses. She then asked for their address and sent them samples.

Although the target audience was comprised of people who she knew already had the problem she was trying to solve, she was surprised to also discover really great design suggestions when they provided their feedback.

Principle 2: Anticipate the Post Pitch

Anticipate and prepare for the post-pitch: Most everyone knows that the initial pitch must be clear, concise, and compelling, but so many entrepreneurs overlook the *post-pitch*. This is when investors ask questions to test your conviction, confidence, and evidence that this is a business worth investing in. In this chapter, you will get insights and inspiration from talented entrepreneurs and how they prepared for the *post-pitch*. They all recognized the significance of answering questions with clarity, confidence, and concision to receive offers from Shark Tank-like investors.

> "Successful investing is anticipating the anticipations of others."
>
> John Maynard Keynes

There is so much emphasis on the pitch that there becomes a tendency to overlook the vitalness of the *post-pitch*. What is the *post-pitch*? It is when you have completed your clear, succinct, and compelling pitch, now the investors are ready to see what you're made of and how you answer difficult questions that will test the viability of your business, product, or service. When I first started pitching investors, I overlooked this critical portion of our investor process and lost out on opportunities by not preparing and practicing answers for this section. Brevity has now launched *Brevity Role Play* which simulates how you answer questions from investors and how to overcome objections in the sales process. Preparation is crucial to hook investors who may not have time or patience to research your methods or draw out your thoughts, you must do that work for them.

The biggest thing I've learned about the post-pitch is even if it's not the correct answer, it's about maintaining your conviction and confidence in these answers. If you don't know the answer to the question, you're better off either telling them you don't know and will get back to them OR telling them your thoughts and asking opened-ended questions to get their opinion. This chapter won't be too long, but it's important to understand that whether you're pitching to investors or pitching customers, you need to be able to overcome common objections to the Achilles Heel of your business model and solution. Objections and questions in the *post-pitch* can feel like someone is attacking you. It's hard to resist being defensive. However, it's truly a sign that someone is engaged and wants uber clarity. Asking questions means your investor is engaged and at least thinking about the problem you're addressing. They're giving you a chance to make a better case. Every time the prospect objects, it's an opportunity to ask more questions and engage in a better conversation about your business.

KATY MALLORY, CEO & CO-FOUNDER, SLUMBERPOD

In our original *How I Pitched This Episode*, Katy highlighted the importance of practicing answers in anticipation of the questions for Shark Tank. Katy and her mother came up with a list of thirty questions from marketing strategy, manufacturing costs, margin data points, and their biggest challenges, to name a few. They also worked with a CFO in her network who they paid an hourly rate to find the critical numbers to memorize for the Shark Tank Investors. Afterward, they made index cards with all of the answers. They categorized which questions her mom would take or which ones she would answer. This was crucial as it's important to show that there's a team and not a one-person solely running the show. As a result, they didn't feel stumped by any questions asked while on the show. They ended up practicing the answers to the *post-pitch* just as much as the pitch. Katy highlights that the key to answering those questions well was being powerful, succinct, energetic, and specific. Your energy needs to remain the same throughout both the pitch and *post-pitch*. Where Katy struggled the most was answering questions about the numbers for her business, specifically when different valuation offers were thrown out. Therefore, one of her index cards contained a matrix of the different scenarios that she could memorize (e.g., if the Sharks changed their offer from 10% to 15%. This worked extremely well for her when she was put on the spot).

BRIAN BRASCH, CEO & CO-FOUNDER OF PRX PERFORMANCE

Another great piece of learning my mentor and investor Brian Brasch shared with me was about anticipation questions. I met Brian Brasch through a colleague in my Sales & Marketing Executive Coaching group at Allied Executives (www.alliedexecutives.com). One day a colleague knew my interest in Entrepreneurship and asked me, "Would you want to be connected to a friend of mine who got an investment from Kevin O'Leary on Shark Tank?" I'm like, *duh! Absolutely.*

The first time Brian and I met we were booked for a 30-minute meeting to learn about his experience on Shark Tank. I asked great questions, and he extended our meeting for another hour. I was amazed by all of the knowledge and gems he provided on our call. I hadn't met anyone like him in my career and knew that I wanted him to be my mentor. Two to three weeks after our first meeting, I ended up sending him an email requesting mentorship. The caveat is that I explained the benefit, structure, and what he would gain from mentorship with me. I acknowledged how busy his schedule was and assured him that it wouldn't be a waste of time at all! We would meet every other month, where I prepared and sent him discussion topics that are ringing my bell in advance. These sessions not only resulted in tremendous learning and development as a leader but also landed one of my first investments into my company Brevity. I showed him that I not only heard his advice, but he could see that I implemented it when I shared a progress update. I strongly believe this coachability and tenacity is why he proactively asked to invest when he heard about the concept of Brevity.

During one of the sessions when he was reflecting on his shark tank success, he highlighted the preparation process for Shark Tank. Being a former CPA (like myself), he was hammering on how important knowing your numbers were, this is where entrepreneurs lose deals on the show. I asked him, "How did you prepare for the that?" He mentioned that he and his partner watched every single episode of Shark Tank and documented the questions the sharks asked post-pitched and how well entrepreneurs sufficiently answered those questions. Sometimes people say that it takes hard work to accomplish one's goals. However, I don't think they understand what hard work means and what's the appropriate amount of effort taken to do enough to reach their goals without concrete examples like Brian. Brian's Shark Tank episode aired in Season 7, Episode 19. So, we could say they analyzed and documented a total of 60 hours worth of episodes in preparation. Now that's commitment toward achieving your goals!

Brian and his partner, Erik Hopperstad documented, grouped, and then made sure they could answer the most commonly asked questions by investors. Then they categorized who would answer each question based on the type of questions. Below is a snippet of the questions they prepared. This rigorous preparation process was absolutely well worth it.

Being clear, succinct, and compelling is critical. These entrepreneurs prepared and practiced answering the questions below as a part of their overall program and it paid off big when they received an investment from Mr. Wonderful, Kevin O'Leary.

TABLE 1: BRIAN BRASCH (BB) AND ERIK HOPPERSTAD (EH) POST-PITCH QUESTIONS

STRATEGY

What is your business model?	EH
How do customers purchase your product?	EH
What percentage of your customers are repeat customers?	EH
What are your social media metrics?	EH
How are customers currently finding you?	EH
How many SKU's do you have?	EH
Who is your biggest competitor and why are you better?	EH
How much of your own money have you invested in the business?	EH
How does this business scale?	EH
Are you willing to send production offshore?	EH
How will your product be distributed?	EH
How big is your market?	EH

FINANCE

What are your sales projected to be this year?	BB
What are your sales for the next 5 years?	BB
What is your sales growth rate?	BB
Are you profitable?	BB
What kind of valuation are you putting on the company?	BB
How did you come up with that valuation?	BB
What will you use the funds for?	BB
How much debt do you have in the business?	BB
How much equity do you have in the business?	BB

TABLE 1, CONTINUED: BRASCH AND HANSON POST-PITCH QUESTIONS

FINANCE, CONTINUED

How much inventory do you have?	BB
What is your monthly SG&A?	BB

MARKETING

What is your customer acquisition cost?	BB
What are, or is your biggest weakness?	EH
What is your marketing strategy?	BB
What is the cost of your core product?	EH
How much do you sell them for retail?	EH
How much do you sell them for wholesale?	EH
Do you have distribution?	EH
Who is your target market and how are you reaching them?	EH
What have been your biggest challenges?	EH

LEGAL

Is your product unique?	BB
Are there others like it?	BB
Is it patented?	BB
What does it cover?	BB
Do you have any other patents?	BB
Can this technology be licensed?	BB
How many total owners are there?	BB

PERSONNEL

What are your backgrounds?	EH/BB

PERSONAL

What do we bring to the table?	EH

ROBBIE CORDO, ENTREPRENEUR COACH

Running a pitch software company like Brevity with aspirations to become the number one pitch software in the world requires credibility, years of experience, and expertise. I can honestly say that I obtained some gifts from God, but I've only been a startup founder for less than two years. I don't know it at all and would be foolish to believe I can democratize the pitch process without working with experts. Recently, we started working with expert business Coach Robbie Cordo (www.robbiecordo.com) when it comes to successfully pitching angel investors. Robbie was a savant in the space and has been a big help to us.

Robbie has had a lot of expertise with the *post-pitch*. He highlighted that conviction and thoughtfulness were 90% of the battle in communicating with investors and answering their post-pitch questions. Below is a tool inspired by many of the practices I learned from Robbie.

As we are on a mission to democratize the pitch for the world, we recognize that nothing beats the hands-on coaching someone like Robbie can provide. He's accelerated our fundraising goal of $1M within a timeline of under 3.5 months so we can get back to focusing on the business. I'm confident that he can do the same for you. Make sure you reach out to a coach like Robbie if you want help perfecting your pitch for fundraising and sales.

TABLE 2: ROBBIE CORDO INSPIRED POST-PITCH TOOL

BASIC REASON BUSINESS EXISTS

Vision—What do we want to create? Why?

Mission—Translate that into business success terms.

Goals—How will we know when we get there; and that we are making progress?

Value Proposition—Who cares that you &/or your product/service exists and what will they pay?

"Elevator" message.

What "pain" is being addressed?

Is this "top-line" or "bottom-line" pain; or does it enable an entirely new mode of business?

What are potential buyers doing today to address this pain?

Is there 3rd party market validation from prospective buyers, industry analysts, channels?

TARGET MARKET(S)

Buyer Profile including buying motivations and openness to new technology, or new methods.

Target market(s) size and forecast.

Market validation.

New product category vs. existing category?

Competition. Does market growth allow company success without displacing incumbents?

How much existing inertia must be overcome for buyers to switch?

How does the critical business issue being addressed by the product rank among buyers' other "distractions"?

PRINCIPLE 2: ANTICIPATE THE POST PITCH

DIFFERENTIATED TECHNOLOGY

Revolutionary vs. evolutionary?

Key differentiators vs. the norm. i.e., is it compelling for someone to consider switching?

Any significant risks to technology completion?

Who owns the technology?

Is it patentable? Are patents meaningful?

Risk of infringement on existing technology (Freedom to Operate).

Is it maintainable in a cost-effective manner resulting in high-quality products?

Is technology dependent on 1 or 2 key players? Are they "locked up"?

PRODUCT DEVELOPMENT (MARKET DRIVEN?)

What is the engineering philosophy and associated processes?

How strong is the project management?

How does engineering interact internally, and with marketing, sales, manufacturing, and service?

Is/was manufacturability a design goal?

What are the standard testing procedures?

PRODUCTS/SERVICES

Product benefits categorized as must-have vs. should-have vs. nice-to-have.

What are direct product costs and associated revenue model.

How are products specified? Are they 'market-driven'?

How often must they be customized?

How are they packaged, distributed, and installed?

TABLE 2, CONTINUED: ROBBIE CORDO INSPIRED POST-PITCH TOOL

SERVICE/TRAINING/MAINTENANCE

What is the process, cost, and revenue model for each?

How was pricing determined?

GO-TO-MARKET STRATEGY

What is the strategic marketing plan?

What is the tactical marketing plan?

What is the product positioning?

How was product price determined?

SALES STRATEGY & REVENUE MODELS

Sales Traction.

What are the distribution methods? Who are the initial targets?

What alliances are in place and are they high-value or low-value?

What is the profile of a strategic partner? How many are there? Who are the main ones?

What are the international plans for distribution? When do they cut in?

What are the revenue models for both direct & indirect sales?

Is there a direct sales force and what is the comp plan?

Reference sites?

COMPETITION INCLUDING BUYER INERTIA

Who are the major competitors and what are the market shares and projected growth rates?

What are the "whole product" strengths and weaknesses against each major competitor?

What are the barriers to entry? How many months' head start is there?

Are there any revolutionary technologies on the horizon? Disruptive technologies?

MANAGEMENT TEAM (EXPERIENCE, BREADTH, DEPTH)

Overall staffing strategy.

Resumes, references, self-evaluations.

Employment and non-compete agreements, if any.

Compensation plans and company ownership.

Is team focusing on wealth creation for themselves and investors?

Is one a "domain" expert in the target market?

Personally and professionally capable of executing their vision.

Amount of cash management has invested, in addition to "sweat equity"?

FINANCIALS (HISTORIC AND PROJECTIONS)

Financing strategy.

Capitalization detail.

Pre-money valuation and justification.

Detailed list of investors and debt holders.

P&L since inception.

Budget for next 18 months including assumptions.

Bottoms-up 3-year revenue and expense projections including methodology and assumptions.

OPERATIONAL PROCESSES

Current financials, especially cash status.

Current liabilities.

Aging A/P.

Operating plan until this round of financing is completed.

TABLE 2, CONTINUED: ROBBIE CORDO INSPIRED POST-PITCH TOOL

LEGAL STATUS AND ISSUES IF ANY

Current or Pending litigation?

Non-disclosure and assignment of rights agreements?

Independent contractor agreement with non-disclosure and assignment of rights.

Beta test agreement, if applicable?

Standard products and services agreements?

CURRENT FINANCING DETAILS

Estimated valuation and method(s) used.

Business plan.

Use of proceeds

How much will retire existing debt?

List of likely new investors. Commitments from existing investors.

EXIT STRATEGY (WHAT'S IN IT FOR THE INVESTOR?)

Similar companies that have existed previously?

Acquisition? When and why? List of candidates.

IPO? When and Why?

BREVITY'S ANTICIPATION QUESTIONS & PROCESS

Obviously, the questions you will get asked are contingent on what you present. For each slide I present, I try to think about three to five questions that may be asked if I were the investor. You also have to consider the short attention spans, low comprehension rates, and zoom fatigue of your target audience.

PRINCIPLE 2: ANTICIPATE THE POST PITCH

As a result, things you may have presented could be asked again. Don't get upset if it happens. This is human nature. The best way to offset any repetitive questions is by ensuring your pitch is as clear, succinct, and compelling as possible. What I've done is list out all of the questions and write out answers with Brevity's (brevitypitch.com) timing logic between 15-30 seconds. Our software has a feature called *Pitchback* that allows you to video record and practice your pitch and answers to commonly asked questions. From here, you can seamlessly send your pitch and other documents to peers/mentors to receive feedback. Below is a list of the questions we've accumulated answers to in 2021. The key is practicing these enough so that your pitch is smooth and confident as it rolls off of the tongue. Please note that it's impossible to be prepared for every single question you may be asked. The point is to prepare yourself enough to build the stress tolerance when dealing with the unexpected questions that will happen.

1. What happens when tech giants create what you're building? How would you categorize the risks and how do you plan to address them?
2. Walk us through your Serviceable Addressable Market (SAM) & Total Addressable Market (TAM)? How did you justify assumptions?
3. Walk us through an overview of your go-to-market strategy.

4. What makes your product unique?
5. What does your team bring to the table?
6. How does your company get to a billion-dollar valuation?
7. What's your gross margin percentage? How do you plan to improve it?
8. How do you justify your current valuation?
9. What's your customer life-time value?
10. How are customers currently finding you?
11. Why would a customer return after one usage?
12. How does this company scale?
13. How do you hit your first-year revenue target?
14. What's your current IP and how do you plan to defend and protect it?
15. What does growth look like in the next five years?
16. Walk us through your current year to date financials.
17. What are your biggest competitors and what makes you different?
18. What are your team's biggest challenges and how do you plan to overcome them?
19. What's the vision of your company and why?
20. What's your target market and why?
21. Walk us through your business model.
22. What are you currently using the funding for?
23. What's your monthly SG&A?

24. What's the end output/outcome/benefit of your product?
25. What's your current customer acquisition cost and how do you plan to improve this?
26. What does hiring look like in the near term and future?
27. What's your exit strategy?
28. What's your churn rate?
29. What are your sales projections this year?

I learned a very difficult lesson in not being prepared while working in my management consultant career under my boss Jonathan Shiery. He drilled us on the significance of anticipating the questions from and patterns of clients, bosses, and colleagues. If you stumbled upon a certain type of question from a client or boss, it's okay.

The point was that you should add this to your toolkit so it's less likely you stumble upon this type of question again. The same goes for pitching for startup fundraising and even the common objections you face when it comes to selling your product or service. Don't get discouraged if you get stumped. Just add the question to your list of common objections and responses.

Moreover, if you start to get repetitive questions, I'm a big fan of adding these within the initial pitch.

There's a concept in storytelling called the Achilles Heel that I learned from my favorite book on pitching called *The 3-Minute Rule: Saying Less To Get More* by Brant Pinvidic. Basically, the Achilles Heel concept is that you proactively bring up the biggest doubt or skepticism in advance. What's the biggest reason why you won't succeed? Acknowledge it head-on, and then briefly discuss how the issue was addressed and how you either solved it or plan to overcome it. Besides this concept, the key lesson is to ensure there is solid logic behind and most importantly, conviction in what you are presenting.

Principle 3: Know Your Audience

A lot of time pitching your business for investment dollars and even to customers is about pitching to the right audience. If I'm pitching Brevity to a cryptocurrency investor, it doesn't matter how much traction I have. If it doesn't fit their investment strategy and focus, it's a waste of time.

> "Who is your number one problem, not what."
>
> Geoffrey Smart

It takes a lot of upfront work, but it's critical to have five to seven criteria of what you consider the right investor. You must be disciplined and focused on creating the requirements criteria and hold yourself accountable for identifying and prospecting your target audience. In this chapter, we highlight how entrepreneurs build their target list and how they secure appointments with their target audience.

My favorite sales and fundraising equation is

$$\text{Results} = \text{Right Investor (Customer)} \times \text{Quality Interaction} \times \text{Quantity}$$

The purpose of this chapter is to deal with the "Right Investor" side of the equation. Let's take each variable and define what they mean and decide the top three considerations for each component of the formula.

"Right investor" means that you're pitching to the right person. Ask yourself, is this investor an active investor with the liquidity to invest now? Does this person have a track record of successful exits and experience within your sector and business model? Just a few initial thoughts. But simply stated, are you pitching the right people?

"Quality Interaction" boils down to your salesmanship from a technique perspective. Do you have a clear, concise, and compelling pitch—basically the purpose of Brevity (brevitypitch.com). Secondly, and super important to me when thinking about quality interaction is *how* you ask the right questions. There's a

PRINCIPLE 3: KNOW YOUR AUDIENCE

concept in Sandler Sales System called, "Qualify hard, to close easy." How effective are you in asking the right questions to move the conversation in the direction to secure funding. The third component of the quality interaction is how effectively you can build rapport and bond with prospective investors. People are investing in you and not just your business. How well you can find common ground and humanize this commercial conversation is an important tactic.

The last portion of the equation relates to quantity. In one sentence, you need to determine if you are pitching to enough net new investors to increase the chances of securing an investment. Principle Five will get more into the weeds of this part of the equation.

Over time, this principle has become just as or more important than the actual elements of crafting and delivering your pitch. If I'm pitching Brevity to a cryptocurrency investor, it doesn't matter how clear, concise, and compelling my pitch is. It's the wrong audience!! I would become so triggered by this early on and even today in my investor prospecting and pitching. I am completely in my feelings when deep down, I know that I'm not taking the time to build out a target list.

Throughout the remainder of this chapter, I will highlight Brian Brasch's high-level approach when thinking about pitching the right fit audience. Then, I'll outline our process, pitfalls to avoid, and best practices from our Friends & Family round to our current $1M raise in 2022.

Something I learned from Brian Brasch's approach to pitching the Right Investor is that before you begin pitching, it is vital to create a Right Investor grid with the following criteria:

1. Stages of financing (Pre-seed, Seed, Series, etc.)
2. Expected Revenue & Metrics
3. Vertical (Finteh, Healthteach)
4. Preferred Business Model (Direct to consumer, Enterprise etc.)
5. Narrow down the focus on the ones who fit & start prospecting.

Even though you want to get your product/service/business idea in front of whoever will listen, it can be a pain to waste time pitching to investors that just aren't right for you and your business. If you're in the day to day operations with running your business, it will be easy to overlook successfully executing your Right Fit Investor grid.

What made it worse for me was that it was extremely hard to sit down and conduct research-based activities (my extroversion is super high). I'm great at connecting the dots and creating hypotheses to test out but I hate doing research for extended periods of time. That being said, once I started being laser focused and disciplined about WHO I'm researching and pitching to, our results drastically improved.

OUR APPROACH TO THE FRIENDS & FAMILY ROUND

For our Friends & Family round, our goal was to raise $200K in capital but we ended up reaching $232,150. Our three primary sources of capital were:

1. Members from the Allied Executives Business Coaching group I belonged to for four years.
2. Peers and Professors from Villanova University.
3. Parents of the kids I coached at Waldron Mercy Academy (the grade school I attend from Kindergarten to eighth) during my grad school program.

With all three places, I had no idea that I would ever be starting my own business that eventually required me to raise capital which is nuts. I've always tried my hardest to be kind, humble, tenacious, and a giver first. While we exceeded our goal, people were astonished when I told them how many investors I pitched within my network. We pitched over 130 investors and landed 16 in our friends and family round.

At first, the process wasn't easy. When you recall our story in *Introduction: Learning from Failure*, I thought I would be able to raise all of the capital needed from Brian Brasch and Wade Rosen for a total of $500K. This wasn't the case at all. When Wade turned me down on the investment, I had to go back to the drawing board. At the time, I honestly believed they were the only wealthy investors in my network who could write a check for my startup. Wade told me, "Kelvin, I know you have other people in your network who could write a check that you haven't even thought of yet."

As always in our relationship, Wade makes me think critically. I got on my whiteboard at my office in Wayzata, Minnesota, and asked myself "Who's mind, heart, and wallet have I positively impacted in my life?" It started with ten names; eventually, the list grew to over 100. I went into the time machine from K-8, high school, college, grad school, coaching, and various roles in my career. I asked my parents who would be good candidates in their network.

Now, if you take 16 divided by 130, that's a 12% close ratio which isn't bad if you consider that a 10% close ratio is considered good. This was a lot of pitching that also cost me a romantic relationship. So be sure that if you're dating someone, you get aligned and on the same page about how time-consuming and stressful this can be on your relationship.

BEST PRACTICES & LESSONS LEARNED FROM FRIENDS & FAMILY ROUND

I'm incredibly proud of what was achieved in this friends and family round. I'm fortunate that my parents sacrificed putting my siblings through private schools in Philadelphia (the public school system isn't the greatest, to say the least). This upbringing opened up doors that gave me an edge in raising capital.

There are some great things that happened from this round and some lessons learned I'd love to share.

Lesson 1
We pitched over 130 investors to actualize our goal in 2021. I strongly believe we assertively outreached and pitched the vast majority of the sphere of influences in my network. One time, I was at a bar in Wayzata and overheard a group of men talking about Artificial Intelligence. I respectfully jumped in and said, "I'm not trying to butt into your conversation, but I couldn't help but hear the words Artificial Intelligence. I happen to run an AI company." I eventually landed three pitches from that meeting.

Lesson 2
We constantly refined our pitch and anticipation answers based on feedback received. This is both good and bad because not all feedback holds the same weight. Now, if I'm getting feedback on

my pitch from someone who's never raised money and invested money into startups like mine, why the hell am I listening to their feedback. This is something I eventually learned that not all feedback is good feedback. No different than you're pitching your target investors, you should be filtering the feedback you're receiving from the right people. Create a list of 5-7 criteria points on who you should receive feedback from and be disciplined determining which feedback to use and which feedback to disregard.

Lesson 3
Research, identify, and pitch more pre-seed institutional funds that write check sizes greater than $100K. Our average check size was $15K at this stage which was great. But it requires way more volume. We had a functional product with users, and we weren't at the idea stage. We could have pitched more funds like Right Side Capital (rightsidecapital.com), they eventually became investors in our $1M funding round). At the time, I wasn't aware that there were funds that actually write checks when you have limited traction but do have a functioning product. I would have at least attempted to pitch 20+ first check funds. I, fortunately and unfortunately, have a strong bias toward taking action. As a result, I didn't enjoy researching, but doing so would have significantly helped our efficiency and process. Slowing down to move fast, as my mentor Matt Raskin (www.linkedin.com/in/matthewraskin) highlights, is essential.

Lesson 4

Scan Key LinkedIn Connections by filtering VC & Private Equity/Angel Investors and ask for warm introductions within your sphere of influence. Again, knowing the criteria of who your target investor is makes it easier to scan for who you will need to be introduced to. Additionally, you can ask, "Anyone in your network who would be interested in Brevity?" This isn't a good question because with all the stress and shit people have on their minds, you require them to burn mental calories to figure out who in their network could help. Even if you hire someone to build a target list based on your criteria, do it! It's worth it. Stop pitching people that don't even deserve to hear your pitch because they're not the right fit.

Lesson 5

Certain Pre-Seed Angel Investors have Seed & Series A Criteria. Many angel investors in the Twin Cities have similar criteria to seed funds in town. I wasted too much time and got mad for no reason because they weren't the right audience to pitch Brevity.

TARGETING FOR OUR $1M ROUND & PROCESS

Since we're in the middle of our $1M raise, we're applying best practices and lessons learned from our previous raise. Below is an outline of the sequential steps we're taking to ensure we're pitching the right audience with a quality pitch and the right number of investors.

Working with Robbie Cordo or other experienced entrepreneurs who've done this before helped us shorten our pathway to fundraising success!

One could make an easy assumption that because we've built a company that helps with honing and perfecting pitches and presentations, we don't need any outside advisors or help. This is far from true. I've been told that *vulnerability breeds innovation.* Influencing, persuading, and presenting are a few of the skills that can always use sharpening. Therefore, we thought it was crucial to work with experienced professionals with a track record to aid us in our fundraising efforts and in ways to improve our own software's effectiveness.

Create Your Right Fit Investor Criteria

This is something I'm proud we've refined. One of my favorite quotes regarding fundraising efficiency is those who chase two rabbits, catch neither. Not everyone deserves to hear your pitch. The first criteria point we flagged as important in the stage of financing category was that we're at the pre-seed stage. I've run into multiple situations where we've pitched a seed investor during the pre-seed stage which ended up being a waste of time for both parties.

PRINCIPLE 3: KNOW YOUR AUDIENCE

The second piece of criteria that was super important was the expected revenue of the investors. For us we're keen on seeing phrases like "Evidence of paying customers." We've always run into issues when we pitched investors expecting $10,000 in monthly recurring revenue. Whether you are pitching angel investors or Venture Capital funds, it's critical to research beforehand, whether online or connecting with founders they've already invested in to get as much information and insights as possible.

The third piece of criteria we identified as a match was what verticals and/or sectors they invested in. Some firms said they're "generalists", but my experience showed that this was usually far from true. Sometimes funds had their most recent investments on their website and/or they have their thesis clearly laid out. At Brevity we were looking for investors with a track record in Messaging Software, Sales Enablement Software, and Communications Software.

The fourth piece of criteria was identifying the investors' preferred business model. Brevity is an enterprise Business-to-Business Software (known as "B2B"). Subtle but a slight difference than Business-to-consumer or direct-to-consumer.

The fifth criteria that was critical for us was the strength of relationships with the type of prospective customers and decision makers within our go-to-market strategy. I'm a firm believer that a lot of your sales success (on top of having a consumer grade product) is contingent on the strength of your relationships. It was important for us to have investors who could provide value outside of just capital.

The next criteria point we were looking for was whether Venture Funds have a BIPOC founder focus. We considered this one a "nice to have" instead of mandatory. There are a ton of statistics that highlight how less than 1% of Venture Funding goes to BIPOC founders. We are fortunate to have Brown Venture Group, Bronze Valley, and Lightship Capital believe in us and make sizable investments in Brevity.

The last criteria piece we identified as a "nice to have" was if the investor had a passion and/or credibility in pitching, presenting, and persuasion. We would research whether these investors had blog articles, books, and Ted Talks on the subject matter. Conducting this research was great because these investors would easily align with our mission and vision of Brevity.

Build a Target List
Once we laid out the strategy mentioned above, our next step was to build out a target list. Building a target list of greater than 50 Pre-seed funds from sources like Signal NFX and cross reference the above criteria. We've built an excel with the following columns:

A. Fund Name
B. Pre-seed Focus (Y/N)
C. Check Size Greater than $100K (Y/N)
D. BIPOC Focus (Y/N)
E. Investment Thesis (Top 3 consideration for investment)
F. Made investment in comparable verticals (Y/N)
G. 3 comparable companies in Sales Enablement, Communication Tech, Marketing Technology
H. If so, what companies? (Name 3)
I. Preferred way to apply and get in touch with firm
J. Linkedin profiles of 2 partners & 1 associate
K. My LinkedIn Connections to Partners & Associates

Establish Connection

Next, I would check if I had any connections to the folks I want to get in contact with via LinkedIn.

If I did have a warm referral, I would send over a double opt-in (meaning both parties agreed to be introduced before the introduction is made) introduction email with the template provided below.

WARM REFERRAL EMAIL TEMPLATE

> Subject Line: Intro to Name for Brevity Fundraising
>
> Name,
>
> Would you be open to introducing me to Name? With their investments in Sales Enablement SaaS (e.g., Company 1 & Company 2), we believe they will resonate with our investment opportunity. Please share the following to gauge their interest for an intro.
>
> Company Overview: Brevity is an AI-powered software which helps professionals craft and deliver persuasive pitches and presentations that sell. Brevity has helped countless organizations raise millions in capital, grow sales, and upskill pitching and presentation capabilities.
>
> Brevity snapshot:
> - Helped founders raise over $5M in capital since 2021
> - Closed $75K in revenue for 2022
> - Raised $500K in capital since 2021
> - Launched MVP in 2021 with over 200 users
> - Won MN Launch Innovation Award in 2021
>
> Brevity Investment: We're raising $1M pre-seed round with $400K committed.

If we don't have a warm referral, I execute the following sequence with the two partners and one associate at the Venture Capital firm.

1. Make sure you either apply through their online submission process or review their preferred method of contacting the firm. Some of the firms make this easier to figure out on their website while some aren't as transparent, unfortunately.
2. I suggest sending a LinkedIn Connection request and a short message that has a summarized version of the double opt-in template message previously highlighted.
3. If they accept your LinkedIn Connection but don't respond, I'll follow up with a LinkedIn Message to grab their attention if they didn't happen to read it.
4. If they don't respond to the previous message, I send an email with an abbreviated version of the double-opt in copy above.
5. I usually follow up one more time via email if I don't hear a response from them after five to seven business days.
6. Lastly, if I genuinely believe they're strong value alignment, I cold call their number to get an appointment. As many successful people believe, "closed mouths don't get fed."

Pitch With Intention

Once you secure the meeting, it's time to crush the pitch and anticipation questions. However, outside of pitching your business, it's critical to walk away with clarity about how their investment process works, who makes the decisions, and how/when investment decisions are made. Again, it's critical not to waste time in the investment process here. My goal is to get the next appointment/follow-up scheduled on the calendar before leaving any investor or sales presentation.

1. The first step, if the investor is interested, is to request access to Brevity's data room. Being an east coaster with nothing to hide, I proactively make our data room available to them via Citrix to so they have access to all of our organizational docs. This is a critical step where they review all important legal, accounting, business plans, investor presentations, cap table, etc. Do not skimp on getting a top-notch startup attorney. We love and recommend leveraging professionals like Doug Ramler at Saul Ewing, who has over twenty years of early-stage startup experience as an attorney. Doug and the firm have been amazing in setting up our incorporation documents and as well as being there for us emotionally during some of Brevity's darker times.

2. The next step of the process is to receive a decision from the investor on whether they want to invest. Once I receive a yes, I shoot over a copy of our SAFE Agreement for the investors to sign. Y-Combinator is a prestigious startup accelerator that popularized the use of SAFE agreements for early-stage fundraising. You can read more about SAFEs at www.ycombinator.com/documents.
3. Once the investor has signed the SAFE agreement, I immediately send the instructions to wire the money into our Wells Fargo account. Don't let the signing of the SAFE agreement and verbal commitments give you false hope. Unfortunately, since starting Brevity, I've had over five SAFE agreements signed with nothing wired into the account. Frustrating, I know, but it's part of the game. Ensure you're tactfully being assertive by following up to ensure you're getting the funds wired into the account.
4. Find the right investor (don't skip this step!). This part of the approach has proven to be most important when getting the bag. The shotgun approach is inefficient. I urge you to slow down first so you can have greater velocity later. If you need to hire someone to help you create the target list or with the entire process, it's well worth the money. Being strategic and diligent about creating a right fit investor list, saves time, energy, heartache, and money. It's not about what, it's about who!

Principle 4: Incorporate Your Motivation

Find your motivation: The startup journey is an uphill one, so it's critical to have motivational sources, routines, and rituals to get back up after you get knocked down. This chapter will highlight motivational stories from our journey and other entrepreneurs on resilience—what it is, why it matters, and how to get it.

> "They don't get too discouraged when things go wrong. They stay motivated. Startup is a game where you're going to fail all the time . . . they stay passionate about the problem, passionate about trying to find a solution, they keep executing and moving forward."
>
> Michael Seibel, CEO Y-Combinator, *What Makes the top 10% of founders different?*

While all of the sections are important pieces of successfully pitching investors, I believe this one has the most significance beyond pitching investors.

Within Seibel's quote above, anytime it says "startup", you could interchange that with *life*. I've always heard the startup game is holistically a marathon, but you need to be prepared to run sprints for extended periods. The main question is how to sustain motivation and not get burnt out. How do you not get too discouraged when things go wrong? I've never experienced so much rejection until raising capital for Brevity. It was a challenge to stay motivated and keep my head up. But what makes things worse is the energy vampires that don't believe in your vision. Surprisingly, if you don't choose your inner circle personally and professionally wisely, this can be your biggest barrier to success.

In the second part of Seibel's quote, "they stay passionate about the problem, passionate about trying to find a solution," the keyword is *passion*. I strongly believe there needs to be an initial baseline for any sustainability, growth, and longevity. One of the interesting concepts I've fallen in love with recently is career clarity. We spend so much time in our vocations (even more than with our family in terms of hours), and I believe it's essential to have that clarity which I feel our education system struggles to give us proper guidance. If you're looking for one of the best career clarity coaches in the market, I highly recommend working with Maggie Mistal (www.maggiemistal.com). I went through her program, and it was clear that running and building Brevity was something I needed to be doing. Sometimes I feel people look to start a business or search for a job for the money as the primary factor. I believe this is an incomplete assessment. Maggie's program walks you through three critical phases to clarity:

1. Soul Search
2. Research
3. Job Search

An overwhelming theme here is being process-oriented pays tremendous dividends. As with anything in life, nothing is black and white. When you deeply understand your interest, skills, motivations, talents, personality, ways to make a difference in the world, and overarching goals of your career, it makes the decision of what company to start, or careers are best suited for you.

I believe the most important piece to staying motivated is to know who you truly are and be unapologetic about it. Surround yourself with a team that will amplify your strengths and cover your weaknesses. When you know yourself—your motivations, skills, field of interest, etc.—selecting a passionate business is easier. Don't skip the process to understand who you are and your field of interest. When the times get tough (which they will), you will need this passion and the right team to supply your gas tank when it's on E.

Motivation is a tricky one as it works differently for all people. As my CEO coach George Flowers (www.linkedin.com/in/george-flowers-6295901b) highlights, you need to find your jazz. Everyone is wired differently, so it's imperative, through trial and error, that you find out what works best for you. It's rarely one thing that motivates us. Depending on the season and time, it may change. Below I want to highlight what works for me and what worked for entrepreneurs I know in my network. As I wrote this passage, my entire founding team resigned making me the remaining founding member at Brevity. To Make matters worse, I was dumped by my girlfriend while recovering from COVID. I was devastated and overwhelmed by the news, but I still strongly believe in the power of Brevity, SOUL and all the things we're developing. This situation definitely knocked me off of my rocker and the wind knocked out of. But I wouldn't quit (at all).

At times, our support circle can be the best motivator. I want to share the story of a father-son duo, Lee & Tripp Phillips from the company Le-Glue. To give some background, they received an offer from Kevin O'Leary on a shark tank. Tripp was a fourth grader with a great idea. The pain that Le-glue's solution addressed was how vulnerable Lego projects are, often

PRINCIPLE 4: INCORPORATE YOUR MOTIVATION

times leaving a hard day (or multiple days) or work to be broken due to simple human clumsiness. A child can especially be heartbroken after their Lego project breaks. Tripp & his father Lee created an adhesive glue to put on your Legos that prevents them from breaking if they happen to fall. Genius concept!

Initially, when I started Brevity, we planned to interview entrepreneurs for a podcast called *How I Pitched This*. The podcast "How I Built This" by Guy Ruz was supposed to emulate this but focused on how they prepared and delivered a pitch that received funding from shark tank investors. We had Lee Phillips on the podcast where we asked about the conception of the business, validation steps, preparation for the pitch, and successes/failures post-shark tank. I asked Lee the question, "Where in your pitch did you all struggle, and how did you overcome?"

Lee responds by telling me a story about his son Tripp, and what they experienced once they got to the popular TV show Shark Tank. He said Tripp didn't seem nervous at all leading up to the show, and even demonstrated exceptional pitching skills while they were practicing. Once they got to the show Lee could tell that Tripp was beginning to feel the pressure. On the set of the show they were called up, suited with mics and then they were on. Lee described his son looking disheveled as the big doors on set swung open and they prepared to meet with the famous investors. Tripp told his dad he didn't think he could go through with the pitch, and Lee said that was the only time his son had any problems during the whole process, so he got down to his son's level to face him and, getting slightly emotional he told Tripp, "It's okay. You got us here. You got us to the Superbowl of business. You've done the whole thing. If you can't speak when you get out there, just look at me. I'll take over your speech. If you fall down, I'll pick you up. One thing you need to understand is there's nobody better to have your back than your dad and I've got your back."

Finally, Lee described to me the turn in this event when his son clenched his fist and said, "Dad, I got this." And when they got out there in front of those investors Tripp didn't miss a beat! He overcame it and received an offer of $80K from Kevin O'Leary. Lee described one of his favorite moments on the episode being when his son made fun of Kevin for not having any hair.

Sharing stories of triumph over challenges is always helpful to build motivation, so here is a list of some of the sources I go to find my motivation: *A clear understanding of your WHY?*

Simon Sinek wrote a book on this, and his book starts with *Why?* I've had the opportunity to see Simon speak live on this topic, and it was very helpful. When I started Brevity, I didn't have a clear picture of my why, and it became more apparent as certain investors asked me deeper questions about our why.

PRINCIPLE 4: INCORPORATE YOUR MOTIVATION

Over time, I discovered the core line which was, "Entrepreneurs constantly pitching, feeling rejected, and overlooked contributes to burnout." There have been times in my life where I've felt overlooked, but what's even worse is being misunderstood. This is why I started Brevity. I grew up the only chip in the cookie at predominantly white private schools. I frequently felt overlooked and misunderstood whether socially, intellectually, or even in athletics. I found growing up in West Philadelphia, around mostly African Americans and being predominantly in a white world in my private schools, was difficult for me to fit into both places. Being an extrovert but not socially accepted in either environment took a toll on my self-esteem and self-worth. As a result, it was a struggle to stay motivated to perform at my best in many aspects of my life. I scored poorly on my SATs and my self-esteem was at an all-time low. Without getting into a pity party, the pain of being misunderstood and overlooked was the fuel and my reason for founding Brevity.

When there's an opportunity to present an amazing idea, I want to increase the chances for people to be clearly understood and engage their audience in wanting to learn more. When there are low points within the journey of Brevity, it's been helpful to reflect on why I'm building this. I believe everyone has a compelling story. We want people to have clarity, confidence, and conviction in who they are, along with communicating in a way that's easy to understand and compelling.

Simon Sinek is one of my favorite thought leaders when it comes to having a strong belief system. Simon has a YouTube video called *Courage Comes From Trust*. In the video, Simon discusses a debate about whether courage comes from internal or external. He strongly believes courage comes from external parties and it's based on the quality of your relationships. He makes the analogy of someone walking on a tightrope and that the reason they have the courage to do so is because there's a safety net at the bottom in case they fall. If you fall, you won't die. The safety net represents the quality of your relationships. The story of Tripp and his father embodies this principle.

For me, my parents, mentors, friends, and investors have faith in me and have my back. I feel loved no matter the outcome is, and having their love and support made a world of difference overcoming the challenges I'm going through (girlfriend breaking up with me, COVID, co-founders resigning, etc). This gave me the confidence to take substantial financial and career risks. When I debated working for someone else or starting Brevity, Wade Rosen said, "Kelvin, you're 31 years old. You're going to regret not doing your own thing. The time is now, and I believe you have something here."

The conviction, confidence, and sincerity of this statement were one of the major reasons why I started this company. Easier said than done because you need people who can provide constructive criticism, but you also need people from whom you can feel their spirit, soul, and energy and know that they have your back. I struggle taking constructive criticism from people that are brash, poor delivery, but great insights. My preference is to collaborate with people that grasp the concept of the emotional bank account in relationships. I've encountered certain people that have a substantial amount of success and talent. However, the delivery and tonality of their feedback doesn't feel like it's coming from a place of love.

This being said, you shouldn't exclude these people from your life if you feel this way because their feedback can be invaluable and take your game to the next level. Make sure that you're consciously surrounding yourself with people and resources that help you perform above and beyond.

CULTIVATE RELATIONSHIPS WITH PEOPLE WHO BELIEVE IN YOU

Continuing from the previous section, I want to highlight a story from Gary V, a popular thought leader in entrepreneurship, marketing, investing, and many other things about successful and authentic living. In this YouTube clip, he highlights how his Spanish teacher knew Gary was going to rule the world even though he was getting Ds in her class. She told Gary's mom that even though she was failing him, she knew he was a special kid who had gifts. This clip is super meaningful to me as it's human nature to give it to the critics and skeptics of what you're trying to build and that's it's not possible. Moreover, people can also get under your skin and tell you you're never going to be shit. And some may have come from circumstances where we literally don't have people who love and believe in us, so this may not be possible. It is important to seek out and invest in genuine relationships to build a circle of support.

CULTIVATE A HEALTHY RELATIONSHIP WITH YOUR BODY & MIND
Body
I've tried a variety of workouts throughout my life and they have had their pros and cons. During my college football days, sprints and agility drills until I puked (at least 15 times playing college football) weren't uncommon. Additionally, I was max squatting 500 lbs., benching 225 lbs 18 times, had a 34.5 inch vertical with a max bench was 315lbs. After football, I completely lost the desire to lift weights. I recognized that lifting weights without heavy anaerobic workouts made me bulky but also made me much angrier as a person. Therefore, I became super interested in training for 5K and 10K charity runs. I never had a strong urge and desire to run a marathon. Perhaps my short attention span, unwillingness, and boredom to create that long playlist contributed to it. I went through a phase of doing yoga, spin

classes, and boot camp classes at the New York Sports Club, Orange Theory, F45, etc.

I began trying out a new program called FightCamp. FightCamp is an interactive at-home boxing workout & equipment and essentially the Peloton for Boxing & Kickboxing. The Rocky movies were a staple while growing up in Philadelphia. We loved the grit, tenacity, and fever that made us our city. One of the favorite quotes that I keep above my heavy bag in my apartment comes from the film Rocky, "The world ain't all sunshine and rainbows. It's a very mean and nasty place, and I don't care how tough you are, it will beat you to your knees and keep you there permanently if you let it. You, me, or nobody is gonna hit as hard as life. But it ain't about how hard you hit, it's about how hard you can get hit and keep moving forward. How much you can take and keep moving forward. That's how winning is done," (Rocky Balboa, 2006). I find this particular quote powerful and motivating as I deal with the many blows that come at me throughout my startup journey. From internal team conflict, constant rejection from investors, and days I'd rather just sleep in because I'm completely drained. I look at this quote and it keeps me going.

All the workouts I mentioned were great, but boxing and kickboxing with FightCamp became not only my favorite workout but symbolic of how I viewed my startup journey with Brevity. Here's why I decided to invest in boxing workouts and why it works for me.

Sometimes our greatest strengths can be the reciprocal of our greatest weaknesses if we don't have a plan to curb them. I've always been someone whose assertiveness could be both a blessing and a curse if I wasn't conscious and present. Boxing five days a week was not only symbolic for me in my journey, but allowed me to be tuned in and to show up my relaxed best self more days than not. I was able to be my *relaxed best self*.

David Allen has a quote in his book *Getting Things Done* which says, "Your ability to generate power is directly proportional to your ability to relax." In a nutshell, this is the end benefit and outcome for me with boxing.

Throughout my life, I've relied too much on brute force to achieve my goals. As a CEO of a SaaS company, your business will fail if you rely entirely on brute force. Similar to boxing, you need to know when to be on the offensive, stall, or be on the defensive depending on the situation. Boxing has become so essential to me remaining level-headed that I compare it to the pill package our elders have from Monday to Sunday. It's problematic if I don't get my dose on Tuesday. To show up and take the daily punches that the startup journey throws at me, I need to be dialed in. Another great acronym that I've been introduced to was the concept of taking your MEDS (Meditation, Exercise, Diet, Sleep). When I'm feeling drained, I think about whether I've taken my MEDS or if I need to change my prescription.

Mind

I'm someone who puts in my heart and soul. I come to the field with a lot of energy and passion. This is a blessing and curse because it makes me vulnerable to the phrase of experiencing the highest highs and the lowest lows. When I started getting coached by George Flowers at *Invisible Hurdle*, he quickly noticed how angry and pissed off I could get in certain situations at the flip of a switch. Lots of emotions can be good, but only if they're used as fuel versus interference. He suggested that I ask my therapist what it took to become a *Professional Emotions Processor*.

A professional emotions processor is someone that can swiftly process emotions and ensure they're leverage as fuel instead of interference in their professional and personal lives. George knows how my brain works and that I could benefit from a system or process to make these emotions become fuel instead of interference. The goal of our coaching is for me to show up 90% of the days, my relaxed best self. When I went to my therapist Jillian Hopkins, she highly recommended a journaling technique called RAIN (Recognize, Accept, Investigate, Nurture). This tool reminds us that our emotions are not who you are, but they give us information about how we are experiencing the world. To help me determine precisely what feelings I'm experiencing, I've used tools like mood meters, or any type of emotion wheel, these are examples of visuals that help identify different emotions that we may be experiencing. If we do a hypothetical example of using RAIN together, it would look like this.

- R—I recognize that I feel tired and fatigued right now.
- A—I accept that I feel tired and fatigued right now.
- I—Perhaps I've been over-extending at work and in my social life (maybe drinking too much alcohol).
- N—This work I'm putting in now is something I'm passionate about and will help enhance the way people create, deliver, and comprehend information. I'm proud to continue to pursue my passion and dream, and it is ok to rest when I need it.

This exercise may seem simple and mundane. But when you truly get accurate about your emotions and flesh them out of your head, it's equivalent to needing to go to the bathroom badly, and you've been holding it. The trick is to have a strong self-awareness of when you're experiencing triggers of high magnitude and to process them as they come in. You don't want to sit on these negative feelings too long because they can have negative side effects on your mental sanity and could lead to a higher propensity of lashing out at other people. RAIN has been an exceptionally useful tool. I used to do this as a part of my morning routine but eventually only started using it on an ad hoc basis. Using this method when I need it the most has been more effective.

Substance Control

This is a heavy and deep topic and a touchy subject, but I felt it was important to discuss, at least from my perspective. My relationship with alcohol as I've gotten older has changed. In my teens and early 20s, it wasn't uncommon for me to have a 10+ drinks nights and then study four hours for my CPA exam and be fine. Additionally, or maybe I didn't notice, the negative emotional and physiological effects it had on my mood and pleasantness. Currently I'm 32 years old, I'm now aware that alcohol without moderation set me back financially, psychologically, emotionally, physically, intellectually, and much more. Because drinking excessively had become a deterrent to my success, I determined my moderation limit based on science and for 375 days, I drank less than with the assistance of an app called Drinker's Helper (www.drinkershelper.com). I now use a different application called Reframe which is similar. I recognize this topic can be a slippery slope, but it wasn't wise (at least for me) to stop learning. And it was important for me to make sure that going beyond my limits didn't interfere with my dream. The common theme throughout this section is understanding what becomes interference versus fuel.

Sleep

What's ironic about this chapter is that I am writing this after having a bad sleep. I woke up at 2 AM with tons of things on my mind about the business. I attempted to put on a stand-up comedian via Netflix with a sleep timer to help me go back to sleep, but it didn't work. My mind was racing with thoughts about my ex-girlfriend while also thinking about business issues. What eventually helped me get some better sleep was that I recognized that I needed to process the strong emotions causing my mind to race and keep me awake. As I mentioned, the RAIN method works best for me when those emotions and triggers have piled up. Therefore, I got out the notepad on my iPhone and started journaling the core emotions contributing to my racing thoughts. It worked, and I eventually gained an additional three hours of sleep. I slept through my alarm and woke up at 7 AM and got on my way to the gym to complete a six-round kickboxing workout to start the day off on the right foot. Admittedly, I'm very disciplined about my morning rituals and routines but less so when it comes to night routines. That said, when I get a strong 6.5 to 7 hours of sleep, I feel like I can conquer the world in the morning. I'm not a sleep hygienist but I noticed a significant difference when I consistently get a great night's rest. There's only so much we can focus on improvement wise. Mastering and improving my sleep regimen is something I will work on in the near future.

In a post-game interview, a reporter asked Lebron James why he thinks he had been so effective over these past few games. Lebron credited his inspiration to being able to watch his eldest son Bronny play ball, he also mentioned REM sleep. In a video from 3CB Performance, Dr. Rajpal Brar, DPT explains what REM sleep is and how utilizing this kind of rest has helped with the longevity of athletes such as Lebron. Two noteworthy things: One is that Lebron is externally motivated by his son, which speaks to the topics of people that believe in us as mentioned in the courage section. Additionally, he's getting the restoration that fuels his motivation. We can all learn from "the King" and take our sleep and restoration seriously. If this entrepreneurial journey is comparable to a marathon, then we want to take a page from Lebron James' approach on taking our sleep seriously.

Quarterly Recharge

Continuing to burn the oils is not only detrimental to your health but will have serious ramifications for your business. I've been a member of the country's largest regional executive business coaching group called Allied Executives (www.alliedexecutives.com). In one of our meetings, we discussed the topic of burnout, I learned the power of the *minimum quarterly recharge*.

Essentially, the idea is that whether you're having a staycation or a vacation, you take minimum of three non-weekend days to unplug from all of your work task completely.

As I was writing this paragraph, I had time plugged into the upcoming weekend to recharge. I was debating on heading to Florida before it got too humid to spend some time with my cousin David Collins. The purpose of recharging is not only to recharge your batteries, but hopefully, to come back with inspiration and insights that will take your business to the next level.

Higher Power & Spirituality

I saved the best for last here as my faith has gotten me and my family through many trials and tribulations, even when I thought there was no way of getting out of them. Life has moments of randomness, but I do believe in the signs and people that God can bring into your life. The purpose of this section is not to push Christianity or any other religion on you, just to express how my faith in a higher power has gotten me through. Getting on my knees at the beginning and the end of the day has had a grounding effect on me. I usually pray for God's protection of my home, family, friends, and myself. I believe there are a lot of dangers and bad spirits out in the world so protection is one of the most important things that I consistently pray for. Secondly, I understand the significance of putting others before yourself, so I usually go into specific prayer requests for people in my inner circle.

Lastly, I ask for blessings, insights, wisdom, and courage for challenges ringing my bell in high intense moments and circumstances. One of my favorite sayings in the Black community is, "It takes a village to raise a child." I also have a church accountability partner, Katherine Johnson, who helped me conceptualize this book and is an investor in Brevity. Our goal is to attend church at least twice a month. We go to Saint Paul Lutheran Reformative Church. It's a very small intimate church where the 8 AM mass has less than ten people. The service isn't too long, and the sermons are interactive, which makes the message stick as you head into your week.

Principle 5: Pitching is a numbers game

Pitching is a numbers game: It's rare that you'll receive a check from the first ten people you pitch. This chapter tells the story of famous entrepreneurs and their pitch tales. Successful entrepreneurs may pitch to hundreds of investors and more. To sound fresh and confident requires lots of practice and repetition.

> "Colonel Sanders, who made Kentucky Fried Chicken famous, pitched his idea more than 80 times before anyone bought the concept."
>
> Grant Cardone 10X

In this chapter, we explore how successful entrepreneurs practice performing to reach peak performance in front of some of the world's most sophisticated investors, The Sharks. These entrepreneurs are prime examples of professionals who *Don't Fear the Sharks*.

> "Practice your pitch as if you're going to remember it six years from now."
>
> Brian Brasch

At the end of the day, it's all still a numbers game to have the greater chance of getting results. During my consulting practice, I'm constantly preaching Results = Right Fit Investor × Quality Interaction × Quantity. Getting results is truly a combination of those three variables.

When I ask entrepreneurs, who struggle with their fundraising, how many investors they've pitched, and they respond with fifteen, I politely give them perspective of our experience in terms of the quantity it took to reach our goals and I use examples from successful entrepreneurs like Walt Disney and KFC. For Brevity to have exceeded our friends & family round target of $200K, it took us over 130 investor pitches with an average check size of $15,000. Getting this was absolutely brutal but fulfilling once we exceeded our target by $60K.

One controversial topic is the amount of VC capital that goes towards women, and BIPOC-owned companies. A 2021 article by Gabrielle Bienasz, published in the Inc. states that, according

PRINCIPLE 5: PITCHING IS A NUMBERS GAME

to recent studies, in 2020 less than 0.06% of Venture Capital funding goes to Black people (Bienasz, 2021). This statistic is sad but as a Black or women-led founder how you interpret this data is make or break. Do you see this as interference or fuel to achieve your goal? I personally take this statistic as fuel! By being tenacious about how I'm honestly performing. Knowing this is a numbers game, am I pitching enough of my target audiences with a clear, succinct, and compelling pitch? Because even if you have a clear, succinct, and compelling pitch and pitching the right audience, it could be bad timing for them, or they just made their last investment? They could have finished their investments for Fund I and you'll have to wait for Fund II. They could have another sector that's a higher priority and in two months they'll have the bandwidth to get after yours. As a result, you'll want to have more opportunities in the pipeline. But the real question is how many I should have on my target list. We've developed an optimal number of prospects formula if you reach out to support@brevitypitch.com. The key assumption is that you've taken the time to think critically about your right fit investor criteria and also you have a clear, succinct, and compelling pitch.

I'm clearly biased toward action which is why I created this book in the first place. It's important to understand that raising capital is even hard to do for white men. Therefore, we have to look at this game is not for the faint of heart for any professional, regardless of race, sex, and gender. I want you to understand the hard realities but also give you tools, inspiration, and encouragement that you can accomplish your goals. Period.

The second element of the numbers games is how much you're practicing your pitch to the point you've memorized it and made the pitch your own so it sounds natural and smooth, and you can speak with the perfect amounts of authority and openness.

In the next couple of sections, we're going to spend some time analyzing entrepreneurs who've been on Shark Tank and how they prepared.

How many investors did it take for these household brand names to get their first break?

1. Peloton: "I would bet I pitched three times a day for four years," Foley said, recalling Peloton's early days on an April 2019 episode of NPR's "How I Built This with Guy Raz." "Between thousands of angels, we had a hundred angels to get the first 10 million. But in order get a hundred angels at my success rate, I probably pitched 3,000 people, and then the 400 institutions that all said no."[*] (Business Insider, 2019[†])

---
[*] www.npr.org/2019/04/05/710439824/live-episode-peloton-john-foley
[†] www.businessinsider.com/why-peloton-ceo-john-foley-thinks-investors-rejected-him-2019-8

PRINCIPLE 5: PITCHING IS A NUMBERS GAME

2. Disney World: "Did you know Walt Disney was rejected 300 times for Mickey Mouse and his Theme Park?" (Forbes, 2019[*])
3. Adaptive Insights: "According to Digital Trends, Adaptive Insights founder [Robert Hull] was turned down for funding by at least 70 VCs. No one believed people would start storing data in the cloud. Its founder had to cut off his own salary at one point and considered selling," (Forbes, 2019[†])

The point is that you need to expect to hit a large number of funds and investors who could potentially write the first check. These entrepreneurs mentioned above are white males who had to constantly pitch a large number of investors to increase the chances of writing the checks. As discussed in the previous chapter, when you pitch the right investors that is clear, succinct, and compelling, the chance of landing an investment increases dramatically. Next, we will focus on how five entrepreneurs practiced making their pitch sound natural, smooth, and confident.

---

[*] www.forbes.com/sites/jamesasquith/2020/12/29/did-you-know-walt-disney-was-rejected-300-times-for-mickey-mouse-and-his-theme-park/?sh=48146ea64a97
[†] www.forbes.com/sites/alejandrocremades/2019/02/05/these-entrepreneurs-were-rejected-hundreds-of-times-before-bringing-in-billions/?sh=66e741c95c67

BRIAN BRASCH, CEO & CO-FOUNDER AT PRX PERFORMANCE

Brian is a very special person to me. He is my mentor, advisor, and investor in Brevity. He was our first interview on our podcast. One of the key takeaways from the interview with Brian was, "Practice your pitch as you're going to remember it perfectly six years from now." Leading up to pitch with the sharks, to say that Brian and his partner Erik Hopperstad (www.linkedin.com/in/erikhopperstad) practiced their pitch relentlessly is an understatement. It took a total of 10 hours to finalize their written pitch. However, the practice schedule and routine was disciplined and consistent. When they woke up in the morning, they'd pitch it to their significant others. On the way to work, they called each other practicing on the phone until they got to work. During the lunch hour, they would practice their pitch again. Leaving work, they would practice this 90-second pitch again and again. When I asked Brian how many hours they practiced, he said easily over 40 hours for a 90-second pitch. Their episode aired six years ago, and he still knows the pitch until this day.

BETH FYNBO, CEO & FOUNDER OF BUSY BABY

Beth believes that her shark tank experience was successful because she was always active in pitch competitions and demos of her product. She participated in 1Million Cups (www.1millioncups.com), MN Cup (carlsonschool.umn.edu/

mn-cup), and many others to keep her pitch finetuned. She also participated in 16 expos. The repetition made a huge difference. Research organizations like Founder's Live (founderslivemedia.com) where you can pitch in front of people to get the repetition and practice before presenting your most critical pitches.

TRIPP PHILLIPS: CO-FOUNDER OF LE-GLUE

In preparation for the pitch audition in Atlanta, Tripp ran through the pitch 40 times before going to the audition. They had a tight window because they only had a week's notice that they would be getting called back. They utilized every opportunity, even practicing their pitch five times while waiting in the long line at the SunTrust Stadium to present.

KATY MALLORY, CEO & CO-FOUNDER AT SLUMBERPOD

In preparation for their shark tank appearance, Katy and her mother practiced over 50 times, including the pitch and questions that they were going to be asked by the sharks. It was extremely important for them to be in sync because it was an interactive two-person pitch. As discussed in the Anticipation chapter, Katy and her mother prepared a list of 30 potential questions that the sharks may ask. They practiced answering their anticipation questions just as much as their pitch. Their goal was to answer the questions in a succinct, powerful, specific, and energetic manner. The practice regiment was extremely helpful Katy in conquering her Achilles Heel which was remembering the numbers of the business. She was deeply afraid of having to do the math on the spot, specifically, on what their valuation would be if a shark proposed a counteroffer. So, they created flashcards and memorized counter proposals in case the sharks proposed different offers.

BECCA DAVISON, CEO & CO-FOUNDER AT UNBUCKLEME

Within Becca's preparation for the pitch, was the preparation for the performance portion of their pitch, where she had her daughter and mother involved. They had to be cognizant of rehearsing enough with and without her so their daughter wouldn't get too tired. They practiced their pitch over 25 times. The other piece was ensuring that they knew their numbers, data, and anticipation questions from the sharks. They prepared by making a long list of every question they could think of. They watched a number of previous episodes and then categorized the different questions that would help them prepare.

A big part of their preparation process was to invite intelligent friends and family members over who didn't have background knowledge on their business. "Running our books helped me know the numbers off the top of my head, so I didn't need to practice as much," Becca notes. What also helped her way before shark tank was a public speaking course in college where she had to present in front of 50 people weekly. What she remembered was how bad the experience of not knowing the answer to a question posed in the class. She recognized that she never wanted it to happen again. This served Becca well. From this experience, she learned that over-preparing and over-researching were one of the best ways to get it done.

Principle 6: Make sure your pitch has SOUL™

SOUL is one of Brevity's proprietary pitch frameworks. It symbolizes the emotional aspects that work best with storytelling and also captures key themes your audience must know. SOUL is high-level enough to apply across industries. It also provides specific guidelines for you to anticipate and answer your audience's questions in the right sequence. Your audience learns and comprehends best when you put your message in the right sequence and explain it succinctly.

> "Brevity is the soul of wit."
>
> Hamlet, William Shakespeare

In this chapter, you will learn the elements of SOUL and how entrepreneurs have embedded this framework in their pitch.

Here's where Brevity's SOUL Pitch Framework comes in handy, by outlining the essential information your audience must know and in what order. In the SOUL framework:

- S = State target audience & problem
- O = Outline how and why your solution works
- U = Uncover proof & potential
- L = List capabilities & needs

One of my favorite jobs during my career was being a management consultant at Navigant Consulting (now the Guidehouse). I was in their Operational Excellence & Technology Enablement Practice. Consulting is an industry that is known for leveraging frameworks to solve businesses' most complex problems and challenges.

I was first exposed to frameworks when preparing and practicing for the infamous case interviews to land a consulting job. Essentially, an interviewer gave a fictitious or real business problem a client was having. It was my job to ask the right questions to unlock the answers to formulate the right solution. Typically, this was done within 30-45 minutes and to make matters worse, you had to compute some mental math without a calculator (something I dreaded even though I'm a CPA).

However, the power of having a framework is priceless in my opinion. A framework does not have to be extremely prescriptive regarding what you do and when but rather a more principle-based set of guidelines that allows room for flexibility. The main purpose is to align and increase the chances of achieving your goal.

So where did SOUL come from? Coincidentally, Brevity & SOUL were inspired from a quote in William Shakespeare's *Hamlet*. In that play, Polonius says, "Brevity is the soul of wit." I woke up on a summer day, and this quote was stuck my mind. Of all the elements it takes to be a successful entrepreneur, to move through the business world and get noticed, I wanted to sum up and make it easier for people to access and understand. Brevity. I immediately texted my business partner and told him the name of our company was Brevity and mentioned the quote. He loved it right away, and we were set on a company name!

I've always been obsessed with pitching concepts, ideas, and businesses from a very young age. I've read countless books on pitching and presenting that include but are not limited to *3-Minute Rule, Why They Buy,*[*] *Building a Storybrand,*[†] and *Made to Stick.*[‡] Most of these books have Frameworks users can use to increase the chances of being clearly understood and compelling. I want to thank all those authors for their insight and inspiration. Now

---

[*] www.amazon.com/dp/1944335684
[†] www.amazon.com/dp/B06XFJ2JGR
[‡] www.amazon.com/dp/B000N2HCKQ

let's get into SOUL, explain the components, and provide some of our favorite examples within that framework.

S: STATE TARGET AUDIENCE & PROBLEM

Target audience: Who are you impacting and what is your consumer market?

The specific audience's problem: What problem is your product elevating or solving?

Identifying the problem is only one of the most important pieces of the framework as it sets the hook and frames the problem. Mark Cuban tells CNBC, "Entrepreneurs should clearly be able to explain what their product/service is and what problems are solved," (Locke, "Mark Cuban: This Kind of Pitch 'always' Results in 'the Best Deal' on 'Shark Tank'"). Let's take a peek at some entrepreneurs who've done a great job answering these statements.

KYNDO, KELLY MCDONALD, 500 STARTUPS DEMO DAY

"Big Brands and your portfolio companies are gonna lose five billion dollars this year to fraud. Now, what if I told you that numbers just for the sixty percent of all influencer's accounts show at

PRINCIPLE 6: MAKE SURE YOUR PITCH HAS SOUL™

least one form of fraud. And what if I told you that we could solve for it. Hi, I'm Kelly McDonald. I'm the CEO and Co-Founder of Kyndo and we solve for social media's biggest problems, fraud attribution, and content safety. And here's how we do it."

Commentary

This pitch set the hook in the beginning by stating Big Brands are losing $5B a year due to fraud. So, it's pretty clear the problem they're looking to solve right from the jump. Then they pivot to the specific problem with 60% of all influencer's accounts show at least one form of fraud. At the end of the section, it's clear who's being impacted by fraud attribution, content safety, and why this matters. The pitch ends with an excellent transition statement, "Here's how we do it." Now, I'm intrigued to learn more about it.

LAURA MUSALL, CEO, COOL REVOLUTION, 2-MINUTE DRILL PITCH

"I'm Laura Musall and I'm the Co-Founder of Cool Revolution, PJs for women with night sweats. And I'm here to ask for an investment of $100,000 to help us keep more hot women cool. This business began in 2019 with a whole lot of sweat, my own. And I'm not talking about just some beads of perspiration. I am talking about dripping pajama-soaked sweat. I'm not alone. Women have told me that they are so desperate to solve these night sweats, they're cranking the AC to 60 degrees and sleeping with fans and ice packs. I thought for sure there would be pajamas to help, but no... What I found were a lot of heat-trapping polyester pajamas or granny jammies or pajamas designed for thin, young women."

Commentary
This one is powerful because of the vivid imagery used to explain the reason why the business started. Depending on the audience, a clear and visual image of the reason for being is an amazing hook. As a person dealing with the problem of night sweats, you could know that you are not alone in the issue. One suggestion to make this a pitch more impactful is to highlight the number of women who struggle with this problem. However, the pitch does infer that the solution that currently exists in the market only targets thin, young women. This suggests that the product is tapping into a side of the market that is not being covered.

RYAN SYDNOR, CEO, GET GROW, 500 STARTUPS DEMO DAY

"I'm Ryan Sydnor, CEO of GetGrow. GetGrow is redefining the f-word at work now. The problem feedback has sucked since 1954. We're all stuck doing reviews to protect the company from low performers which are only about 10% of a team. The game we play is if I actually like you. And I know my feedback goes on the record and affects your compensation. I'm bound to amp up the positives and tone down anything negative that leaves the

PRINCIPLE 6: MAKE SURE YOUR PITCH HAS SOUL™

remaining 90% of us feeling safe but starving for meaningful feedback that can help us be our best. It's no wonder employees today rank opportunities to learn and grow above compensation when they're deciding where to work. The lack of meaningful feedback is lowering performance and people will get fed up and leave. This is costing companies money which is why the f-word needs to get redefined now. Introducing the world's fastest way to give meaningful feedback to people."

Commentary
Having a strong background working in the corporate environment as a CPA at a Big 4 firm and management consultant, I understand this problem intimately. I love how this pitch highlighted the F word (feedback), which was a great hook to grab attention knowing that this term could be interpreted as a curse word, but he quickly ties it in to feedback. Ryan does a great job of telling a macro-level story of how feedback is currently given and why meaningful results are not collected using that particular process. Ryan is smart for highlighting the fact that employees rank opportunities to learn and grow above compensation. It also adds further magnitude to the problem of not giving meaningful feedback and how not having it contributes to employee turnover which results in companies losing money. Lastly, the pitch provides an exceptional transition to the next phase by stating, "Introducing the world's fastest way to give meaningful feedback to people." I'm now eager to learn how this works.

DEVON COPLEY, CEO, AVATOUR, 500 STARTUPS DEMO DAY

"When all you have is a hammer everything looks like a nail. Zoom is a hammer. It's a terrific tool for the kind of meetings that would normally happen in a conference room but a lot of meetings don't happen in conference rooms. They happen on-site like inspections and audits tours and walk-throughs of facilities and site-specific training. There are over two billion meetings like this every year. With COVID, people have tried to use traditional video conferencing for site meetings but video conferencing was built for faces not spaces. Using Zoom for a site meeting is like using a hammer on cheese. Different tasks require different tools. That's Avatour's remote collaboration designed for on-site meetings."

Commentary

The use of an analogy in the opening is excellent. Visual images help people comprehend the concept and pain quickly. You can assume everyone listening to this pitch knows what type of a tool a hammer is. In this remote world if you haven't heard of Zoom you're going to know what it is now. By comparing Zoom to a hammer as the only option, you can grasp the problem almost before he even says it. And the question is, "Who is the target audience in this pitch?" Who are the people on-site at inspections, audit tours, etc? This pitch also sizes the magnitude of the problem by stating the mass amount (2 billion) of meetings that happen like this annually. My favorite part of this pitch is, "People have tried to use traditional video conferencing for site meetings, but video conferencing was built for faces, not spaces." Not only does this make logical sense but leveraging the use of rhyming is a mechanism to make the pitch really stick. Moreover, the additional analogy, "Using Zoom for a site meeting is like using a hammer on cheese," is relatable and funny. Some would say it's unnecessary to use these analogies, but I would say they don't understand the times we're in. We're competing with short attention spans, low comprehension rates, and zoom fatigue. Leveraging techniques like analogies help make your message stick with the audience. Even as I typed this, I could recall Zoom calls are meant for faces and not spaces. The last statement is excellent and explains the entire value proposition. It also serves as a strong transition into outlining how & why the solution works.

ANTON BREVDE, CEO, ASSETA, Y-COMBINATOR DEMO DAY

"Hello my name is Anton Brevde and I'm the CEO of Asseta. We are the ebay for capital equipment. What that means is we help manufacturers buy and sell used capital equipment and parts."

Commentary

This opener is quick and to the point about who they serve (Manufactures), and you can infer there's a problem with selling used capital equipment and parts. However, this pitch isn't explicit about the pain and magnitude of the need. One thing to keep in mind is that this pitch was two minutes and 33 seconds. When under time constraints it can be difficult to capture every single element of the SOUL framework. This is perfectly okay. The framework is meant to be guideline-oriented and not so procedural. There are some constraints with the framework, but it's meant to drive creativity within the guidelines of it.

KELVIN JOHNSON JR., CEO & CO-FOUNDER BREVITY

"Good afternoon, my name is Kelvin Johnson and I'm the CEO & Co-Founder of Brevity. Prior to Brevity, I launched a new SaaS business unit to profitability within twelve months. Throughout my career, I have failed and discovered what it takes to create a great pitch. We developed a smarter way to pitch. The number one mistake founders make is they can't explain what their business does. This has a negative impact on their ability to raise capital and more importantly, grow revenue. Constantly pitching, feeling rejected, and being overlooked contributes to burnout. There were times in my life where I felt overlooked, but what was worse was being misunderstood. This is why I started Brevity, an AI-powered software helping professionals craft and deliver persuasive pitches and presentations that sell. To best explain how it works, I'd like to highlight the story of one of our users, Sophia Khan, the CEO & Co-Founder of Voythos. Before using Brevity, Sophia was on her way to her first Venture Capital pitch at a Starbucks in Houston, Texas. When it was over, Sophia received feedback that she was too verbose, had missed essential concepts, and could have benefitted from a story. This changed working with Brevity."

Commentary
Kind of weird giving commentary on our own pitch, but let's give this a shot. In the pitch, I quickly attempt to establish credibility from my career experience. Sometimes if you're pitching alongside a large number of other entrepreneurs, you need a hook to grab investors' attention immediately. I learned to have the humility that I've failed pitching throughout my career but eventually discovered the key to delivering a great pitch. I quickly capture the macro-level problem by explaining the number one mistake founders make: they can't explain what their business does. This quote came from an extremely reputable thought leader, Michael Seibel, the CEO of Y-Combinator. I try to elicit emotions by saying, "There have been times in my life where I've felt overlooked, but what's even worse is being misunderstood." One of my favorite books that inspired Brevity is *Made to Stick*. They have the best book when it comes to creating a compelling message. They use a framework called SUCCES: Simple, Unexpected, Credible, Concrete, Emotion, and Story. They analyzed over ten thousand pitches, political campaigns, advertisements, articles, etc. We

explain the problem we're solving in greater detail by leveraging a concrete story from one of our users Sophia Khan and her first Venture Capitalists pitch at a Starbucks in Houston, Texas. Is this Starbucks in Houston, Texas, necessary to communicate? We strongly believe so because this visual image helps make it stick. We then highlight three specific pain points that are product helps solve: 1) being too verbose, 2) missing essential concepts, and 3) needing a story. We end the transition statement that this changed working with Brevity.

O: OUTLINE HOW & WHY YOUR SOLUTION WORKS

How: Walk us through how your solution works

Why: Tell us why your solution is needed. In other words, if your product exited the market tomorrow, what would be missing?

This part of your pitch process is the opportunity for you to provide a high-level and detailed outline of how and why your solution will solve the problem for your target audience. Creating an outline for your solution can be one of the most challenging things because most solutions have multiple steps which, if given all at once, can be overwhelming to the audience. Therefore, it is vital that you break down your plan into sequential, palatable steps that your audience can follow. Below are examples of how other entrepreneurs have crafted this section.

KYNDO, KELLY MCDONALD, 500 STARTUPS DEMO DAY

"Kyndo has analyzed the profiles of more than 80 million follower accounts. We know which ones are real people and which ones are fake bots and our AI understands which influencers they follow and what content they engage with. We're tracking every paid post on the major social networks and scoring its performance. Our audience database scores influencers for authenticity and engagement. While providing brands with insights that go beyond the swipe and our 14-point content safety check looks for posts containing things like profanity, nudity, violence, divisive language or sensitive social topics. Ensuring brands aren't working with the hashtag #fakefamous or worse."

Commentary

Pitches that contain intellectual property are the most difficult because you need to explain why your unique ideas without sharing your secret sauce, but this pitch is a great example of how it can be done. You need to give just enough information for the investor to know you're on to something special without giving up your secret sauce. For AI to be useful you typically need a lot of data, so acknowledging that the company has analyzed 80 million follower accounts establishes your product's credibility. The pitch highlights the outcomes from the deep learning algorithms created. Their process steps include tracking every paid post as well as scoring performance. These scores include authenticity and engagement. I also love how they've mentioned the 14-point safety check, highlighting the more prominent points from that list. The last statement magnifies the critical detail, ensuring brands aren't working with #fakefamous or worse. This goes back to solving the problem of fraud attribution and content safety, and emphasizes the state target audience & problem section.

LAURA MUSALL, CEO, COOL REVOLUTION, 2-MINUTE DRILL PITCH

"My friend Mindy Ford and I decided women deserve better. So, with the advice and input from a menopause expert and researcher from Indiana University, we designed pajamas that help. Cool Revolution pjs are made of bamboo, which we love because it's sustainable, naturally cooling and moisture-wicking."

Commentary

This was for a 2-minute pitch, so this section had to be relatively short. That being said, the pitch mentions that they utilized input from experts and researchers to design pajamas that solve the problem. The Indiana University piece adds name recognition and provides credibility. The last piece answers both why this product is needed and why the materials used are essential: "it's sustainable, natural cooling, and moisture-wicking." By the end of this portion, I understand at a high-level how and why the solution works all which was done in three statements.

RYAN SYDNOR, CEO, GET GROW, 500 STARTUPS DEMO DAY

"Install our slack app for free in seconds. What you see here is why everyone loves GetGrow. GetGrow's feedback flow, our templates help you overcome writer's block and submit in under two minutes. We've achieved product market fit and have started going viral. GetGrow already been installed by over a thousand teams across 62 countries including companies like Netflix, IBM, and Ebay since joining 500. We've grown mrr at 300% and just hit 6k. And we've done all this without spending a cent on marketing. Here 's how we land and expand."

Commentary

On top of being succinct, GetGrow had a strong video to accompany their pitch. The pitch clearly walks you through the sequential steps: 1) Install the Slack app for free in seconds. (I love the use of time measurement because we all want quick and easy). 2) They mention the drop-down templates to create feedback. 3) Submit in under two minutes. Altogether three easy steps to provide high quality feedback without experiencing writer's block. Now I'm thinking, "Damn I want to try this!"

The pitch then expands on the value creation and why it is needed. The mention of achieving product market fit and going viral is just what investors want to hear. What's more impressive is that the app has been installed by over 1000 teams in 62 countries and by marquee brand names (again, name recognition and credibility). The pitch provides impressive MRR (monthly recurring revenue) growth of 300% & hit 6k users. Lastly, the pitch hits home by emphasizing organic growth before jumping to the plans to achieve product potential in the next section. Credibility has been established that could be used during the uncover proof and potential portion. This pitch does an exceptional job of answering how & why the solution' works.

DEVON COPLEY, CEO, AVATOUR, 500 STARTUPS DEMO DAY

"We're a SaaS platform that uses off-the-shelf 360 hardware to deliver full context of the remote site to users anywhere in the world. Either in browser or using an optional VR headset, either way users can speak with the folks on the other side and be able to accomplish tasks almost as if they were there getting the job done without travel. For the very first time now when you have the right tool you've got customers."

Commentary

This pitch does a great job of quickly explaining how, and maybe more importantly, where this is happening. I've come across certain pitches, and wasn't unsure whether the product was available via mobile application, web platform, etc. That's not good if people don't understand the physical location of where you're adding value after your pitch. I love that this pitch offers two options and then follows up with "getting the job done without travel." This distinctly outlines the value proposition of the product, especially during COVID times. However, I'm not in love with the transition phrase to the next section. I wasn't sure what the pitch was getting at there. It is always important to make sure your direction is clear.

ANTON BREVDE, CEO, ASSETA, Y-COMBINATOR DEMO DAY

"Here's a great example of what we do. In 2001, Oakley paid two hundred twenty four thousand dollars for this optical coder. They were done using it and it was just sitting in their warehouse collecting dust. We helped them get it onto our website and in less than a month. It sold for forty thousand dollars. Now our initial target market is high-tech manufacturers. Last year they spent 14 billion dollars on used capital equipment and parts. Overall a hundred billion dollars is spent each year on used capital equipment. We are going to bring all of these transactions to one online marketplace. But why aren't they already online? Well people have tried creating capital equipment market places. But they took the wrong approach. There were two much like ebay. They thought that they could just create a website and manufacturers would come posts equipment on their own. That doesn't work as manufacturers are not incentivized to post equipment on their own. The secret to making this marketplace work is to focus above all on mechanisms for getting the inventory."

Commentary

I always preach that one of the best ways to make your product stick is by provide a testimonial of a customer who has used your product. The formula goes: the customer's problem before your product, the process using your product, and the outcome/benefit after using your product. Asseta does an amazing job with this section. We used a similar format with our Brevity pitch that I will highlight as well. Moving on, they focus on the market size of used capital equipment and parts at 14 billion dollars, which plants the seed for how large this market is. Again, Venture Capitalist's desire a large market size. They transition with questions like "Why aren't they already online?" This is a great hook because, up to this point, there doesn't appear to be anything special about Asseta's model. As we think about the "why the solution works" portion of this section, this pitch hooks the audience with an open-ended question. Essentially, without giving away too much information, they allude to their secret sauce, that they've figured out how to obtain the inventory from the manufacturers.

KELVIN JOHNSON, CEO & CO-FOUNDER OF BREVITY

"When Sophia logged in, she first selected her pitch goal and duration, where our software's timing logic recommends the number of statements and slides to keep her pitch on time. Next, she created her pitch script with our SOUL™ framework, which allowed Sophia to capture Voythos' core concepts in a story like fashion. To give you some background, SOUL is a framework we trademarked: the S is state target audience & problem, O is outline how & why solution works, U is uncover proof & potential, L is list capabilities & needs. Sophia improved her content by working through Brevity's Pitch Intelligence.™ Next, she identified what was missing by working through our peer feedback system. With the last step of our software, Sophia finalized her slide content in our SOUL framework. She then polished her designs working with Pitch.com. This is an important distinction between how our company differs from most competitors. Those companies are hyper-focused on slide design, layout, and formatting while Brevity focuses on story, content, and message development. Brevity prioritizes substance over form."

Commentary

We believe that telling a story of singular, concrete, and inspirational character makes the problem, product, and end benefit stickier. Using SOUL to pitch SOUL was no easy task. People assume pitching a pitch company is like clockwork for us. This is far from true. It's actually easier to help others craft their pitches than ours. That being said, we want to slow down and make sure we explain the framework and acronym thoroughly. If you notice, the pain points identified in the previous section are pretty verbose, missing essential elements, and needing a story, we address steps to solve this in the *Outline How & Why it Works* section. Drawing a line from our ideas and tools to how we stand out from the competition was important. It clicked for certain investors when we ended with *Brevity prioritizes substance over form*. We've had a lot of challenges being associated with being a pitch deck company. We actually provide storytelling as a service and sales messaging as a service. Therefore, lines like *substance over form* are important for us to verbalize and visualize so our target audience can grasp how different we are from our competitors.

U: UNCOVER PROOF & POTENTIAL

Proof: How do you know (testimonials, patents, revenue growth, etc.)?

Potential: Tell us where you're going (horizontal growth, market size, etc.)

Arguably this one of the most critical sections of the SOUL framework. People need to clearly believe with absolute conviction, confidence, and supporting evidence that what you've pitched in the S&O section is believable, concrete, and credible. With any lack of confidence and strong information, your pitch won't survive. This goes back to the importance of the first principle: Validate your key assumptions. Secondly, the importance of explaining what your potential is but more importantly, how you plan to reach your potential effectively is critical. The first part is a clear understanding of what the potential is, but where I've struggled in pitching is clearly outlining how you'll get there with confidence, conviction, and defendable logic in a concise manner. You have to have this mapped out to a tee! In this section, we'll continue with examples of how entrepreneurs crafted their narratives.

KYNDO, KELLY MCDONALD, 500 STARTUPS DEMO DAY

"Now brands of all sizes are already trusting our data including large enterprise brands like Pillpack and Minted and direct to consumer brands like Pluto and CannaCraft. Our north star is for brands to be able to plug into our data and predict the influencers that will drive commerce. We see influencer marketing as our wedge into the global predictive analytics market. Getting there will require an experienced team."

Commentary
Since this is a quick pitch and you need to draw engagement for someone to learn more, Kyndo does an exceptional job of hitting proof & potential quickly. This pitch answers the proof theme by mentioning the four well-known brands to establish quick credibility. I also love how they use the phrase "north star" to transition into the potential portion of the pitch. Basically, the north star metric is a popular term in the Venture Capitalist circle that demonstrates vision and focus. Lastly, I love the mention of influencer marketing as the wedge into a larger addressable market with a global predictive analytics market. This is significance because Venture Capitalist want to see initial focus but they want to invest in companies that can compete and dominate a huge market. However, they understand that you can't capture the entire market right away and it needs to be done in phases.

You can't be everything to everybody. Or, as Confucius says, "The man who chases two rabbits, catches neither." Using a word like wedge paints the picture for a possible expansion in the future. While investors want to see the vision, at the same time they must see your focus. Ending with "getting there will require an

PRINCIPLE 6: MAKE SURE YOUR PITCH HAS SOUL™

experienced team" is the perfect transition into the next portion of the pitch. Transition phrases are super important, as well as pausing. This is because people need time to comprehend what's been said before you jump to the next idea. Since we're competing against short attention spans, low comprehension rates, and Zoom fatigue, allowing the audience to keep up is critical. Kyndo does a great job of this here.

LAURA MUSALL, CEO, COOL REVOLUTION, 2-MINUTE DRILL PITCH

"We've sold them to women in every state in the country online. We've been in "Forbes," "USA today," "Women's World" magazine, but most of all, women are telling us they're helping them. But the need is so great. There are 20 million women in the U.S. in menopause. And according to the national menopause foundation, 1.3 million women enter menopause every year. The average age is 51. This problem is not going to go away. And it lasts for a decade or more."

Commentary

I love how this pitch gives evidence in this section. The list goes:

1. Sold to women in every state online. The online piece is great because she's providing specificity of the medium of where their product is sold.

2. We've been in Forbes, USA Today, and Women's World Magazine. Highlighting the publicity and recognition received from well-known publications is also another great validation point for certain audiences where endorsement and ambassadors are meaningful.
3. The most important proof point is that women are telling them this actually works.

These are unbelievable proof points and based on what I heard, I would like to learn more. As we transition to the potential portion, the pitch does a great job of communicating the serviceable, addressable market with 20 million women experiencing menopause. The pitch also highlights a strong secondary research point by mentioning the National Menopause Foundation. Lastly, to drive home the potential, the stickiness of this product is addressed by emphasizing that this problem isn't going away and can last for up to ten years. Not only does this product solve the problem of night sweats, but it is clear the company has done their home and knows its market/domain very well. This pitch is a stellar example of uncovering proof & potential.

RYAN SYDNOR, CEO, GET GROW, 500 STARTUPS DEMO DAY

"Word of mouth is causing our distribution channels to take notice. For example, Slack featured us right alongside google and zoom as a top three apps. When employees start using and loving Grow, I simply loop in HR, show them real engagement metrics and close deals on our pro plan. And that's why we're winning. People actually use GetGrow. Users get 20 times more feedback than with our competitors and that feedback is higher quality too because we tap into the wisdom of the team. Companies spend 9 billion a year to solve the feedback problem and based on our current growth rate, we should hit a million in ARR (Annual Recurring Revenue) this year."

Commentary
In this pitch, Get Grow hits the proof quickly and succinctly. They provide a killer example with Slack featuring them along with google and zoom as the top three apps. In the digital age, pretty much everyone knows Google and Zoom. A couple of his most important phrases are, *Real engagement metrics* and *Users get 20 times more feedback than with our competitors.* The pitch paints the picture of the sales process to give the investors confidence, not only because the company has perfected their sales process, but with the proof their product works, employees use it, and HR is buying in. In terms of the potential, the pitch does an excellent job stressing how much companies spend ($9B a year) in efforts to solve the feedback problem. One of the most important things I personally struggle with is not only telling investors where I plan to go, but succinctly explaining how. This pitch knocks this element out of the park by stating, "Based on our current growth

rate, we should hit a million in ARR this year." $1M in ARR is one of those milestones most startups never get to, which is very impressive.

DEVON COPLEY, CEO, AVATOUR, 500 STARTUPS DEMO DAY

"Now when you have the right tool you've got customers, eight hundred thousand dollars in ARR in just ten months and a suite of customers that runs the gamut from life sciences to logistics to food production to even government. Now there's a wide variety of applications for Avatour but our target market is inspection certifications and audits, a 210 billion dollar space that spends 14 billion dollars a year on travel."

Commentary

This pitch comes right out with the proof that'll lift your ears. Not only does it provide relatively high annual recurring revenue metrics, but it gives you the short time frame in which this result occurred which is important as you're framing your proof point. Data without a timeframe reference isn't a strong data point. Transitioning to the potential piece is how the pitch highlights the wide use cases from life sciences, logistics, food production, and government.

Additionally, I love the framing of, "now there's a wide variety of applications for our company, but our target market is inspection certifications and audits, a $210 billion space that spends $14 billion a year on travel." Venture Capitalists want to see focus. This pitch gives that focus and a very large market size at $210 billion that spends $14 billion a year on travel.

ANTON BREVDE, CEO, ASSETA, Y-COMBINATOR DEMO DAY

"That's what we've done and it's working over the past three months. We've built a website and collected over 28,000 equipment listings. The results have been great. Revenue has grown two hundred fifty percent month over month. We have two hundred and twelve thousand dollars in sales and we're profitable. This is a huge opportunity with manufacturers spending a hundred billion dollars each year in used capital equipment. With our five percent commission, we have a total addressable market of five billion dollars."

Commentary

This pitch does an excellent job, like in the last section, of explaining the how and then following up with the proof that they've collected 28K equipment listings. They've proven the model works. Taking it a step further, the pitch dives into the proof that Asseta is making revenue at amazing growth rates of 250%. More importantly, the pitch proves that the company became profitable in a short amount of time, ending by doubling down on the expenditure of $100B. The total addressable market of $5B based on the commission rates is a nice touch. It's easy to follow the math, which makes it even more sticky and not too complicated.

KELVIN JOHNSON, CEO & CO-FOUNDER OF BREVITY

"This formula is working as founders like Sophia are securing capital, closing sales, and winning pitch competitions. And to continue the success we achieved in 2021, we signed a contract with the Knight Foundation for $75K. Startup fundraiser pitching is the wedge into a larger market where sales professionals and college students will be communicating with Brevity. To scale quickly, we will sell group license subscriptions at an average annual contract value of $10K.

Commentary

This is actually the part of our pitch that I'm not in love with. As an impatient CEO, I thought we'd be much further along as a product and company. The most valuable service we provide to clients is one-on-one coaching, and the software adds a tool that gives us an edge above the rest. That being said, in the previous section, we ended by saying, "Brevity prioritizes substance over form." For our proof, we ended Sophia's story by highlighting that she secured her pre-seed funding. On our pitch deck slides, you can see that she raised $200K in capital. To add more proof, we added additional entrepreneurs on the slide who have raised capital totaling over $2M in capital since we launched our MVP. We added an element of potential, communicating that the tool has been used for closing sales and winning pitch competitions. We included additional proof by explaining the strategic partnership we closed with the Knight Foundation for $75K. We have over 200 members, but we never turned on the payment portal so that I couldn't bank on any recurring revenue at this juncture. What you'll notice is that you can't make up data. You have to think critically about your proof and speak to that.

In the absence of a strong proof section, you better communicate what your potential is and how you will effectively meet or exceed your potential. In the absence of quantitative proof (the best form), you need to anchor on qualitative proof from your customers and users. As for our potential portion, we state our focus with the startup entrepreneurs but quickly highlight that this tool is relevant for sales professionals & college students in a larger addressable market. Without a strong monthly recurring revenue, I attempted to explain how we reach our potential by focusing on the group license purchase strategy. Honestly, I believe we could do a much stronger job and sharpen how we will reach our potential with more potency which I was in the middle of revising while writing this book. What you'll realize during your startup journey is that you have to work with the data and results you have. However, you can control the narratives by confidently explaining how you plan to achieve your potential.

L: LIST CAPABILITIES & NEEDS

Capabilities: What makes you confident that you're the one to invest in?

Needs: Tell us what you need to succeed.

This section is important, but if I had to rank it against its components, it would be S, U, O, and then L. All of these are mission-critical and must naturally flow from one and the other. When we think about capabilities, a potential investor or buyer needs to know that you're the right person, team, or company to place a bet on. They need to know at a high level how your business operates and succeeds, and specific achievements or accomplishments that confirm for them that you're the right person to invest in. Your listed achievements can't be general like, "I have 35 years in the SaaS business." You could have worked for 35 years but sucked during that time.

Some school of thought, you should spotlight your credibility right from the jump. Investors will pay better attention to the remainder of your pitch if you establish authority and credibility at the beginning. I can say, as a BIPOC founder, this is probably borderline necessity as we're competing against institutional biases. As for the needs portion, you need to be specific and concrete about your offer, ask, or request. For example, let me know if you'd like to know more won't cut it. If it's a fundraiser pitch, the amount you're raising, and the use of funds works.

However, the last portion of the needs definition is success and how you define it is critical. Painting and explaining the vision of that is necessary. If you've ever watched the show Entrepreneur Elevator Pitch, Peter Goldberg is constantly complaining about "Where's the asks?! There's no ask." I've talked enough. Let's continue with our examples.

KYNDO, KELLY MCDONALD, 500 STARTUPS DEMO DAY

"We can do It. *Get it?* Can do. We Kyndo it. Jin and I are the perfect founder duo. I'm a sales and operations expert with a track record in building high performing teams from scratch and a background in data marketing. Jin is a data and AI genius. He's a three-time founder with one exit and was the chief architect at Openx, the world's second largest ad exchange platform. Together we've already onboarded a team of trusted former colleagues. Now if you're interested in predicting the future of social commerce with us, let's chat. Thank you all for joining us."

Commentary

"We Kyndo it," a little humor and puns don't hurt anyone. This can be effective to make your message stick. One of the key influences for Brevity was the book *Made to Stick*.* Dan and Chip Heath analyzed well over 10,000 of the most influential advertisements, political campaigns, pitches, and commercials, etc. They've created, in my opinion, the best equation to make an idea memorable, compelling, and sticky. The framework is called *SUCCES*: Simple, Unexpected, Concrete, Credible, Emotion, and Story. But I digress.

This pitch does an exceptional job of communicating both founders' expertise. But more importantly, it focuses on a high-level and specific element of the founders' track record which could suggest these are the right leaders to build a team by highlighting, "with a track record in building high performing teams from scratch and background in data marketing." We've seen too many pitches where people list years of experience without mentioning something valuable within their track record. Years of experience isn't credible without proof points that you've accomplished success and major breakthroughs.

The pitch does an exceptional job of highlighting her partner within three statements. The speaker mentions the expertise,

---

* www.amazon.com/dp/B000N2HCKQ

but reinforces by 1) naming a credible brand she was a part of, 2) being a startup founder three times, 3) successfully exiting a business. Investors are looking to earn a return, so it's awesome that this isn't their first rodeo. The pitch also does an exceptional job of communicating that the growing team was already onboarded with trusted former colleagues.

Knowing from firsthand experience, it's vital to get the early team right from the jump. Strong and passionate team members are 90% of the battle. Including this in the pitch absolutely makes me want to learn more. Wrapping up the capabilities portion and I would give it a grade of 9 out of 10. Let's move to the evaluate the needs portion.

Traditionally, you'd like to disclose the amount you're seeking in terms of funding. However, during the stream of demo days with this cohort, I believe if the pitch piqued someone's interest, this information will be discussed in the follow-up meeting.

The SOUL framework is guideline based and is not prescriptive. I love how this pitch ends by painting the picture of where they are going in the future, and inviting people to have a conversation, if they're interested, in "predicting the future of social commerce with us." It's rare that you'll close prospective investors after one pitch. Again, the purpose of the pitch is to drive engagement and desire to learn more.

LAURA MUSALL, CEO, COOL REVOLUTION, 2-MINUTE DRILL PITCH

"Will you help with a $100,000 investment to keep hot women cool?"

Commentary

When you're strapped for time like Laura was in this 2-minute pitch, you don't always have the luxury of hitting the 2-part components of each letter of the SOUL acronym. Therefore, you need to make a judgment call about what element will be more important for your target audience based on the context. When looking at shows like 2-Minute Drill* and Entrepreneur Elevator Pitch (www.entrepreneur.com/video/series/elevatorpitch), the investors constantly complain about not knowing what the ask is. Why aren't these entrepreneurs asking for what they need? This pitch eloquently makes the ask while combining the value proposition of the offering, "keeping hot women cool."

RYAN SYDNOR, CEO, GET GROW, 500 STARTUPS DEMO DAY

"Richard and I embraced feedback while leading teams at Epic and Bridgewater Associates before we met in grad school at Cornell. So if you want to help us redefine the f word learn, why we've

---

* www.amazon.com/2-Minute-Drill/dp/B08TB4CHBN

planted over 10,000 real trees, or hear about why people have stopped saying feedback and started saying GetGrow, come join us in our breakout room, 29. Let's grow together."

Commentary
Here this pitch does an exceptional job of highlighting a specific yet high-level detail of what the founding team has done previously in their careers to give investors the confidence they're the right team. Also, highlighting a credible Ivy league grad school program could add benefit. Depending on the audience, facts like these carry a whole lot of weight. Most of the time investors want to learn about how you met your co-founders. Next, the pitch infuses personal passions like, "why we planted over 10,000 trees." This shows that the company is operated by humans who care about the community, which isn't too far from the mission of the company. Lastly, the pitch ends with "let's grow together", a tagline based on the name and purpose of the business. It's a nice hook. Notice that the pitch doesn't highlight the ask but invites interested parties to join a breakout room to learn more. This invitation adds a more intimate element and may be a risk that pays off.

DEVON COPLEY, CEO, AVATOUR, 500 STARTUPS DEMO DAY

"It's this inefficiency that we're going to tackle first. Now an opportunity like this requires an experienced team. I helped build a

SaaS B2B unicorn before. And I have a prior exit as a CTO. My partner Prasad was the lead on the Dolby Vision team and has 12 patent applications. We met working on the Nokia Ozo program. And we've spent five years working side by side. So we have the traction, the TAM, the team, and the right tool for on-site meetings. I'm Devin Copley. I hope you come chat, thanks."

Commentary
This section is all about communicating clearly and succinctly, and with confidence why anyone should invest in you. A lot of times people highlight years of experience, which isn't bad. However, a stronger indicator is stressing key wins achieved within the years of experience. The line, "I helped build a SaaS B2B unicorn before. And I have a prior exit as a CTO," is a wide dose of credibility packed into two statements. Notice this isn't a long list like a resume. This pitch pulled out the most relevant piece of individual success that would give the investor's interest to have a further conversation.

Secondly, the pitch is not only able to highlight notable accomplishments but adds credibility by mentioning Dolby Vision and 12 patented applications. Additionally, a little back story on how the founders met adds a personal touch that could help investors feel more connected to the overall vision. Investors tend to prefer to invest in teams where there's a strong bond and prior work history, so stating the five years of experience together and example of the working relationship could go a long way. As we think about the concept of making things sticky, the pitch ends with a powerful alliteration with the four Ts: Traction, TAM, Team, and Tool. This seems unnecessary, but we're, again, competing with short attention spans, low comprehension rates, and capital competition. It's imperative to make your message and content stick and include what the investors want to hear.

KELVIN JOHNSON, CEO & CO-FOUNDER OF BREVITY

We're currently raising $1M in capital with $400K committed. The expected outcomes are achieving $1M in annual recurring revenue and patenting *Pitch Intelligence*. This puts us in a strong position to raise a seed round of $3-$5M in 2024." And we have the right team and experience to grow Brevity. Collectively, we have scaled revenue and profit and launched successful SaaS products. We believe it will become a common phrase, "Are you communicating with Brevity?"

Commentary
We quickly delve into what we need ($1M) and highlight where we are in achieving that number. Moreover, we jump into what we expect to accomplish with the money invested. We also show that we're thinking about how much money we'll need in the future. We end by highlighting our team's capabilities specifically.

We also wanted to end with a version of our vision by emphasizing the last line of what we believe will become a common phrase, "Are you communicating with Brevity?" Notice that we don't highlight "are you pitching" with Brevity. We aspire to become a communications juggernaut. Why not plant the seed now?

NOW WHAT?

You got a baseline understanding of how six entrepreneurs applied SOUL for various types of pitches. But the questions are what about the pitch decks, and how many slides are based on various pitch types, audiences, and goals? How does SOUL work for my specific industry and vertical? What if my pitch is longer than four minutes? You can find all of these answers on brevitypitch.com, an AI-powered pitch software that helps professionals craft and deliver persuasive pitches and presentations that sell. Enter coupon code NOFEAR and receive 50% off your annual subscription. You get access to over 100 frameworks for high-stakes professional communication, Brevity Pitch Intelligence™ example library, Pitchback, and much more.

Outro & Additional Resources

Thank you for purchasing this book and hearing my perspective on what I've learned so far from other successful entrepreneurs and what's helped us raise close to $500K since the conception of Brevity. We still have a long way to go with so much more to learn. It means the world that you were willing to sift through my first book. Just to make it stick, I wanted to provide a recap of the six principles:

1. Validate your key assumptions
2. Anticipate and prepare answers to investors' questions
3. Make sure you're pitching the right audience
4. Find your motivation
5. Pitching is a numbers game
6. Make sure your pitch has SOUL

I strongly believe these capture tactful, pragmatic, and tangible attitudes, tips, and behaviors to make your fundraising goals become a reality.

Sign-up for an account at brevitypitch.com to help you craft clear, concise, and compelling pitches for fundraising, sales, and internal presentations.

Remember, wisdom = experience + failing forward. One of my favorite equations (yes, another one). The reality is, when it comes to pitching, you need to get yourself in the game of making enough attempts. You get better over time. You have to be vulnerable to accept your failures, learn from them, implement changes, and keep moving forward. You've got this! I believe in you. *Don't Fear the Sharks!*

References

500 Global. "Batch 27 Digital Demo Day." *YouTube*, 4 Feb. 2021, www.youtube.com/watch?v=FcfAi3fAdg0.

Anton Brevde. "Asseta Y Combinator Demo Day." *YouTube*, 3 June 2020, www.youtube.com/watch?v=AGEdHAT_f-k.

David Meltzer. "Episode #1 | 2 Minute Drill Pitch Show." *YouTube*, 13 Jan. 2021, www.youtube.com/watch?v=d6C2UnIYq-g.

Simon Sinek. "Courage Comes From Trust | Simon Sinek." *YouTube*, 29 Oct. 2021, www.youtube.com/watch?v=Wkl3FDxgPdo.

3CB Performance. "Is 'REM Sleep' LeBron James Secret to Success? Expert Explains." *YouTube*, 15 Dec. 2021, www.youtube.com/watch?v=FNF-n7BQAmw.

Bienasz, Gabrielle. "Black Entrepreneurs Are Raising Record Amounts of Venture Capital in 2021." *Inc.com*, July 2021, www.inc.com/gabrielle-bienasz/black-founders-funding-increase-venture-capital.html.

---. "Mark Cuban: This Kind of Pitch 'always' Results in 'the Best Deal' on 'Shark Tank.'" *CNBC*, 7 Nov. 2020, www.cnbc.com/2020/11/07/mark-cuban-which-pitch-results-in-best-shark-tank-deal.html.

Rogers, Taylor Nicole. "Peloton Is Valued at More Than $4 Billion, but CEO and Co-Founder John Foley Says Investors Turned His Pitches Down for 4 Years. These Are the Reasons Why He Thinks They Were Rejected so Many Times." *Business Insider*, 29 Aug. 2019, www.businessinsider.com/why-peloton-ceo-john-foley-thinks-investors-rejected-him-2019-8.

Asquith, James. "Did You Know Walt Disney Was Rejected 300 Times for Mickey Mouse and His Theme Park." *Forbes*, 29 Dec. 2019, www.forbes.com/sites/jamesasquith/2020/12/29/did-you-know-walt-disney-was-rejected-300-times-for-mickey-mouse-and-his-theme-park/?sh=14f2d5a84a97.

Cremades, Alejandro. "These Entrepreneurs Were Rejected Hundreds of Times Before Bringing in Billions." *Forbes*, 5 Feb. 2019, www.forbes.com/sites/alejandrocremades/2019/02/05/these-entrepreneurs-were-rejected-hundreds-of-times-before-bringing-in-billions/?sh=3f636cd05c67.

www.ingramcontent.com/pod-product-compliance
Lightning Source LLC
Chambersburg PA
CBHW012106090526
44592CB00019B/2671